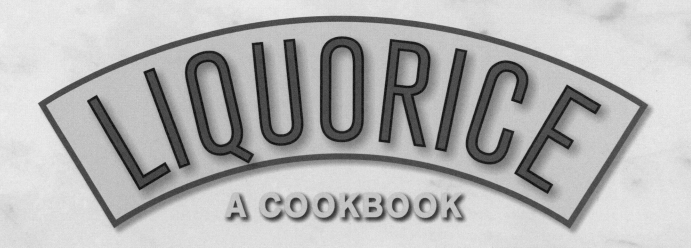

LIQUORICE

A COOKBOOK

**FROM STICKS TO SYRUP:
DELICIOUS SWEET AND SAVOURY RECIPES**

Carol Wilson
Photography by Nicki Dowey

LORENZ BOOKS

Contents

Introduction

The story of liquorice

I have been fascinated by liquorice ever since my childhood deliberations over the enticing sweetshop tray of pocketmoney-friendly shiny, black, soft, pliable sticks, novelty shapes and intriguing woody 'twigs', which are in fact the dried roots. I fell in love with the rich aroma and aromatic bittersweet taste that lingered in the mouth – and quickly became an enthusiastic liquorice devotee.

I often wondered over the years, what is liquorice, where does it come from, and how is it made? It was some time later that my investigations into its origins, together with my love of liquorice, led to my writing this book.

The story of liquorice is astonishing and goes back a long way. The ancient Scythians, Greeks, Egyptians, Romans and Chinese prized liquorice for its health-giving properties, and its original use was purely medicinal and remedial. It still has an important role in herbal and Chinese medicine today. The transition from medicine to confection and its role in national cultures is an intriguing journey through history.

Of course, it's as confectionery that most of us enjoy liquorice, and there's an ever-increasing range to choose from. Liquorice lovers all over the world enjoy their own particular favourite, whether sweet, salty, bitter, or flavoured; perhaps long chewy soft sticks or as hard pellets to suck... along with new kinds of 'gourmet' liquorice and a dazzling variety of unexpected liquorice products including tea, sausages, bacon and even toothpaste.

But liquorice is much more than sweet confectionery; its sophisticated, herbal taste makes it a marvellous culinary ingredient as well. As the main character or appearing in the background, the unique flavour of black liquorice adds a special taste to both sweet and savoury dishes.

In these pages you'll find history, advice, and both traditional and new recipes that will appeal even to people who say they don't like liquorice! Explore how to use roots, sticks, powder, essence and syrups to bring a subtle and truly distinctive flavour to your food.

A WORD OF CAUTION

Even though liquorice has many beneficial properties, and is safe for most people, it is important not to overdo it by eating too much or for too long. The national health guidelines in the UK advise not to eat more than 57g (2oz) a day for longer than two weeks. The active ingredient, glycyrrhiza, if taken in excess, can lead to headaches, high blood pressure, lower potassium and cause water retention or have a laxative effect. Children and people with hypertension, kidney problems, diabetes or heart problems, or if pregnant, should avoid eating too much liquorice. It can interact with some medicines, and it is best to ask the advice of a pharmacist or health professional.

Harvested liquorice roots. *The natural dried root can be chewed as it is, but is also the start of the transformation process into all kinds of wonderful liquorice products.*

What is liquorice?

The unique strong, bittersweet taste of liquorice is unmistakable, and comes largely from *anethole,* a sweet-tasting compound also found in anise and fennel, although the plants aren't related. Purified juice extracted from the roots is used for the culinary ingredient.

The liquorice bush is an attractive small perennial, native to the Middle East, southern Europe and parts of Asia, and is related botanically to peas, beans, clover and lupins. It grows wild on riverbanks in Iran, Turkey, India, Syria, China and Southern Europe and in the wild, the plants grow taller each year, eventually growing to five feet tall. Pretty purple or pale blue flowers appear from June to July, followed by small reddish-brown pods similar to a partly grown pea pod, each containing three or four seeds.

There are over a dozen varieties of liquorice, each with its own particular flavour according to the variety. Some are used in the making of cough mixtures and throat lozenges, and as a way to sweeten the taste of medicines. Glycyrrhiza glabra (the botanical Latin name which translates as 'sweet root') is the most widely cultivated and the most valuable commercially.

The plant is often found under its Latin name *Liquiritia officinalis*, a corruption of *glycyrrhiza*, from which the English name 'Liquorice' or 'Licorice'

(spelled *Lycorys* in the thirteenth century), the Italian Regolizia, the German Lacrisse or Lakriz, the Welsh *Lacris* and the French *Reglisse* are all derived.

The roots are not the only edible part of the plant; the shoots can be eaten and the leaves have been used in small amounts for herbal teas. But it is the roots which are important. They contain *glycyrrhizin*, which is about fifty times sweeter than sugar, but this sweetness is very different from sugar, being less instant, sharp and longer lasting.

Much of the roots' sweetness comes from *glycyrrhizin*, although the exact content of each liquorice species depends on several factors, such as the type of soil, hours of sun and rainfall. The more *glycyrrhizin* the root contains, the higher its quality, but it should be between 6–14%. Liquorice contains bitter substances, which partly mask the sweet taste, as well as vitamins E, B1, B2, B3, B6, B9 complex, biotin, lecithin, manganese, niacin, pantothenic acid, phosphorus, protein, zinc and other trace elements.

Glycyrrhiza glabra *There are different varieties of the herbaceous perennial legume: the common Glycyrrhiza glabra is the most popular for liquorice cultivation.*

Leguminosae.

Glycyrrhiza glabra L.

Liquorice cultivation

Cultivation can be difficult as the liquorice shrub has the traits of an intrusive weed and needs careful management. The crowns or runners are planted in early spring, in deep, well-drained, rich, fine soil with plenty of moisture (this helps the sweet elements in the root to form). It needs a warm climate, as the plant can't tolerate severe freezing, and cold weather also inhibits the development of the sweet juices in the root. Growth is slow – the roots aren't ready for harvesting until the end of the third year, although harvesting generally takes place in the fourth year, by which time the roots are sweet and fleshy. If the roots are harvested too early they will be deficient in sweet components.

The thick fibrous roots are long and reach down into the ground, often with several runners penetrating to a depth of more than a metre or three feet. These runners bear leaf buds and throw up stems in their second year. Both the downward-running roots and runners are harvested. The plant is usually prevented from flowering, to conserve its energy into producing good quality roots. If flowering does occur the sweetness is reduced. The root system is so dense that after harvesting, sufficient root remains in the ground to regenerate the plant.

The arduous work of extracting the long roots takes place in the autumn, once the leaves have died back. To harvest the plant, trenches are dug and the soil loosened, then the roots are removed and the branches trimmed off.

Until the late nineteenth century, Spain grew most of the world's liquorice (hence the origin of the nickname for liquorice, 'Spanish') but today it's also cultivated commercially on a large scale in Turkey, Iraq and Spain. Particularly fine liquorice is harvested in Italy, in the regions of Calabria and Abruzzo.

Liquorice bushes *growing (in Calabria, Italy). A newly planted liquorice shrub will typically take 3–4 years to grow to the size required for harvesting; the thick fibrous roots are carefully chopped to allow for regrowth, and collected for drying.*

Liquorice production

The roots are washed, cut into small pieces, covered and then dried naturally for four to six months, although nowadays mechanical dryers are also used. The dried roots can be stored for long periods without any loss of quality. After drying, the moisture content is reduced from 50% to 10%. The dark outer layer is peeled off some roots before drying; this peeled liquorice is yellow and is used for pharmaceutical purposes.

The cleaned, dried roots are shredded in ten times their volume of hot water (60°C/140°F), usually by centrifuge in machines, and the resultant liquid is left to settle. The liquid is decanted into evaporating pans to be concentrated at a controlled temperature. The extract is then transferred to steam-heated pans or kettles fitted with revolving scrapers.

The evaporation continues until the extract is about 75% of its volume with 18–25% moisture and has formed a pulp. This pulp is filtered and concentrated, then poured into blocks while hot and left to cool and dry to a thick, black tar-like mass. This final product is called block liquorice and has a strong overpowering flavour. The hard, shiny block liquorice is exported to tobacco, confectionery, food, alcohol, cosmetic and pharmaceutical companies for further use. Other extraction methods involve grinding the woody roots to a yellowish brown powder that can be used as it is, or mixed with water.

Block liquorice is dissolved in warm water before using. As block liquorice is approximately fifty times sweeter than sugar, only a little is needed. Liquorice confectionery normally requires about 1–4% block juice mixed with sugar, gums, starch, colouring and flavourings. It's not always black – some liquorice is chestnut brown; nor is it always sweet – the Dutch, Germans and Scandinavians prefer salty liquorice.

Liquorice is probably best known to us today as a confectionery product, but it has many other uses. Its sweet taste is used to mask unpleasant-tasting medicines; extracts are used in the tobacco, cosmetic and brewing industries, in liqueur making, and also to flavour drinks, both non-alcoholic and alcoholic.

Scenes from the liquorice factory:
the concentrated extract is transferred to
a heated pan with a revolving scraper.
As the blades revolve and the mixture
heats up, most of the moisture is
removed. After filtering, the cooked
concentrated paste is left to dry and
set before being chopped.

Growing liquorice in your garden

*L*iquorice is a lovely ornamental plant with pretty, light-green foliage and blue or pale violet and white flowers appearing in late summer (if it hasn't been subject to weather that's too cold), and will establish itself quickly in the garden. In cooler climates the plant rarely flowers. If you want to grow liquorice in a garden, plants are available from most nurseries, but make sure you don't confuse true liquorice with other plants with common names like 'liquorice plant', which is Helichrysum petiolare.

Liquorice is deep-rooting and is best grown in the ground, as it doesn't grow well in containers unless they are large and very deep. The variety 'Pontefract' is a hardy herbaceous plant and will tolerate temperatures down to -15°C/5°F. 'Pozan' is another variety commonly grown, but it's less hardy than 'Pontefract' requiring winter protection in cooler parts of the country. In the USA the edible native plant is *Glycyrrhiza lepidota*.

You can buy liquorice seedlings and seeds from some garden centres; once planted they will establish themselves quickly and become an interesting topic of conversation!

The plants can be planted outdoors once the danger of frost has passed in late spring, after acclimatising them to outdoor conditions for ten to fifteen days. Liquorice plants require a position in full sun and dislike clay soils. They should be grown in deep, fertile, well-drained, moisture-retentive, alkaline soil and planted roughly a metre or three feet apart. They will grow to a height of one to one and half metres (or four to five feet); a deep, alluvial sandy soil encourages the formation of long taproots and a wide root zone, so there's more to harvest. The plants like plenty of heat, which increases their sweetness, and they will grow in Mediterranean through to tropical climates as long as the roots don't stay too wet. They will also tolerate frosts as they die down in winter.

If the plants are grown for the roots they can be harvested in the autumn once the foliage has died back. The first harvest can take place three to four years after planting. It takes about this length of time for the plant to develop enough thick, fleshy roots to harvest, but don't leave it longer than that, as the roots become woody and less palatable.

Lift the plants in the autumn, remove the larger root s required for use, and leave the smaller ones to provide a crop for the following year. The newer smaller roots should be replanted immediately to prevent drying out. The crown is stored: cut the roots away from the crown and store the crowns in slightly moist compost and leave in a cool dark place until spring, when they can be planted out, after all risk of frost has past.

The root can be used raw or used as a flavouring. The cleaned roots can be cut into small lengths, washed and dried and either left to air-dry, then stored in an airtight container, or you can cover the roots with water in a pan and boil them down to make a thick, molasses-like extract. This can then be used in cooking.

Flowering liquorice plant,
Glycyrrhiza glabra.

Liquorice through the ages

*L*iquorice has been in use since the earliest days of history, when it flourished in the wild. Like many herbs and roots, liquorice root was prized by the ancients for its medicinal and health-giving qualities. A large quantity was found in the tomb of pharaoh Tutankhamen (1350BCE) and amazingly was found to be exceptionally well preserved. Egyptians have been drinking erk sous, a drink made from liquorice root (still sold by street vendors in Cairo) for thousands of years, as it's believed to strengthen the immune system. Many Arabs drink erk sous during Ramadan, as it lessens their thirst.

Liquorice roots as well as the twigs, leaves and flowers were used in Chinese medicine as early as 2800BCE and liquorice is still included today. Nearly all Chinese herbal formulas contain liquorice because it assists in gastrointestinal absorption and boosts the effects of other herbs. The Chinese word for liquorice is gan-cao which means 'sweet herb'.

Liquorice root's long and distinguished history as a medicine by the Scythians, Sumerians, Assyrians, Greeks, Romans, Babylonians, Indians and Chinese is well documented. The Scythians, a large group of Iranian Eurasian nomads in the eighth and seventh centuries BCE established a powerful empire and instructed the Greeks how to use liquorice root. Philosopher Theophrastus of Lesbos (c. 370–c. 285BCE) was known as the 'father of botany' and in his Inquiry into Plants called it 'Scythian root' and noted that it was used to treat asthma, dry coughs and chest complaints. It was also valued in ancient Arabia for treating coughs, strengthening the stomach and as a tonic to ensure good health. The Greek physician Dioscorides (c. 40–c. 90CE) was the most important botanical writer after Theophrastus

and it was he who gave the plant its botanical name *Glyrrhiza* (Greek glukos, 'sweet' and riza, 'root'). Dioscorides accompanied the army of Alexander the Great and instructed the troops to take liquorice roots with them to chew to reduce their thirst when water was scarce and to give them strength during their long marches. He also considered liquorice useful for treating stomach, throat, liver and kidney disorders.

Manuscripts from 360CE describe liquorice as relieving skin diseases and coughs. Both Alexander the Great and Julius Caesar advocated the health benefits of eating liquorice and it was an essential part of the rations for Roman legions to build stamina and energy and relieve both hunger and thirst during their long exhausting campaigns. Liquorice is probably the only sweet substance that has this effect; the theory being that chewing the root until all the juice is extracted leaves a bitter taste that acts on the salivary glands to remove thirst. Glycyrrhizin, the active principle in the root, does in fact promote sodium and water retention, consequently reducing the sensation of thirst. This property was also utilised by Hannibal who fed his elephants liquorice when he took them over the Alps; similarly, Arabs on the camel trains across the desert gave their camels liquorice to stop them becoming thirsty.

Wild American liquorice plants (*Glycyrrhiza lepidota*) were valued by Native Americans who used both the leaves and roots for medicinal purposes. The Cheyenne ate the raw young shoots of the plant

Liquorice appears in medieval herbals, such as this 1385 Latin manuscript of Tacuinum Sanitatis, itself translated from the 11th-century Arabic work Taqwim al-Sihha by Ibn Butlan.

Liquiritia.

Nature. F. a. h. in. 2ᵒ. melior exca non nimis grossa et coto
sa. Juuamenti. adens nentutem asperitati pectoris. nocumentu.
si nascetur in terra crexosa. remono nocu. remi plantata in terra sabu
losa.

A long history: Antique photographs of 'erk sous' sellers – the sweet liquorice drink has been enjoyed for centuries in North Africa. Sorting the liquorice allsorts was done by hand in the Bassett's factory. Liquorice was originally sold in the USA for medicinal purposes.

in the spring and made tea from the roots to treat stomach upsets, while the Blackfeet made a similar tea to relieve coughs and sore throats.

In India, traditional Ayurvedic medicine regards liquorice root as an expectorant, spasm-relieving, and anti-inflammatory. Mixed into warm milk it's used as a heart tonic. In Sanskrit it's called yashtimadhu (yashti meaning 'stem, stalk' and madhu, meaning 'sweet'). In Hindi liquorice is known as mulethi.

Medieval European physicians learnt the medicinal uses of the root from the Arabs and Greeks and liquorice appears to have been in general use in England in the Middle Ages. In 1264, liquorice extract was recorded in the Wardrobe Accounts of Henry IV and in 1305 a tax was levied on liquorice imports during the reign of Edward I, to aid in repairing London Bridge.

During the thirteenth century, liquorice extract combined with gum or honey was commonly used throughout Europe as a medicine for coughs and sore throats. In the fifteenth century, liquorice was listed among the commodities kept by Italian apothecaries and was named in a record of drugs of the City of Frankfurt, written about 1450. Later, English herbalists mention liquorice quite often, including the eminent herbalists M. Gerard and Nicolas Culpeper. At the end of the sixteenth century, Gerard grew it abundantly in his London physic garden and at the end of the seventeenth century Culpeper wrote 'it is planted in field and gardens in divers place of this land and therof good profit is made' and recommended its use for coughs, wheezing, shortness of breath, chest and lung complaints. An English medicinal preparation called diapenidion containing liquorice, sugar, pine nuts, almonds, cinnamon, cloves, ginger and starch

was prescribed for chest complaints and this was still in use in the seventeenth century. Jane Baber's 'Book of Receipts' (c. 1625) included using 'juise of licquorish' in a recipe remarkably similar to the later recipe for Pontefract cakes. Her method combined liquorice root, hyssop, rosemary, coltsfoot, water and sugar cooked until thickened, then shaped into rolls.

Cookery writer Eliza Smith in her book The Compleat Housewife, or Accomplish'd Gentlewoman's Companion (1727) gave instructions for 'The Tar-Pills for a Cough': 'Take tar, and drop it on powder of liquorice, and make it up into pills; take two every night going to bed, and in a morning drink a glass of fair water, that liquorice has been three or four days steeped in; do this for nine or ten days together, as you find good.'

The pollution and smog of the large industrial cities of the nineteenth century led to many chest and lung complaints, with liquorice preparations being prescribed to treat these conditions.

One illustrious liquorice devotee was Napoleon Bonaparte. He carried a mixture of liquorice powder and brown sugar as a remedy for indigestion and colds and kept small pieces of liquorice in a tortoiseshell box. When he was dying in 1821, it was reported that one of his last requests was for liquorice-flavoured water.

Liquorice is often used in Moroccan and Asian cuisines. In Morocco it is used to flavour snail and octopus dishes and is an ingredient in the popular spice blend ras el hanout. In Asian cooking it is used in soy sauce, five-spice powder and in marinades and sauces. Ground into powder (jethimadh) it is much-used in Indian cuisine and dried liquorice root is chewed as a mouth-freshener after meals.

A history of liquorice in Italy

In Italy, the regions of Abruzzo and Calabria have been producing liquorice possibly as far back as Roman times. In the sixteenth century the Dominican monks of the Monastery in Atri in Abruzzo began to cultivate and harvest the roots from wild liquorice plants that grew profusely in the region to extract the liquorice juice. Some Calabrian farmers cultivated the plant, but extracting the juice was an arduous process. A writer in the first half of the sixteenth century noted that the liquorice plant was abundant in many parts of Italy and described how succus (extract) was made by crushing and boiling the fresh roots.

This modest scale of production was taken to the next level in 1836 by Rodolfo de Rosa in Atri, who opened a factory to manufacture liquorice, leading to liquorice from the region becoming famous throughout Italy and Europe. Today the two biggest producers of Abruzzo liquorice are centred in Atri and Silvi. Many of the town markets offer a marvellous variety of liquorice including roots, pure liquorice bricks, long ribbed bands and colourful sugar-coated pearls.

Calabria is still one of the major liquorice producers in Italy. The Duke of Corigliano opened the region's first Concio (liquorice factory) in 1715 to extract the juice of the plant roots to produce unsweetened shiny, black liquorice. The harvested roots were stored outside the factory (as they are today), ground by a large grindstone (no grindstone anymore!) and boiled. The juice obtained was put through a sieve or strainer, and cooked in huge pots until the mass was reduced and thickened. While still warm and soft, it was shaped by hand into sticks, tiny buttons and squares.

The factory methods increased production and led to the rise of several famous liquorice companies in the region; probably the best known is 'Amarelli' (1731) still in existence today. The Museo della Liquirizia Giorgio Amarelli in Rossano is a fascinating glimpse into the history of liquorice production methods. Nowadays, juice extraction, boiling and reduction are all computerised and automatically controlled, but the final stage of production is still done under the masterful supervision of an expert 'master liquorice maker' who determines when the black paste is the correct consistency and ready for shaping.

Early in the twentieth century, the market for Calabrian liquorice slumped as cheaper imports led to the closure of many companies. But nowadays thanks to the new Consortium of Liquorice di Calabria DOP and help from the Region Calabria, the production of liquorice is active again and a renewed source of local economy.

The famous Amarelli liquorice factory in Rossano, Calabria has been producing wonderful liquorice products for hundreds of years.

A history of liquorice in France

Locally grown liquorice root was once harvested in the south of France, particularly in Camargue, and the sweet juice pressed from it was mixed with honey and rolled into small balls to treat throat complaints, respiratory illnesses and to aid digestion. As local production failed to keep up with demand, liquorice root was imported from Spain, Italy and the Middle East.

Gradually the medicinal aspects of liquorice gave way to the manufacture of sweets such as cachous and herbal teas. The small town of Uzès in the south of France was the centre of liquorice (réglisse) production. In 1862, Henry Lafont opened the famous Zan liquorice factory in Uzès known today as Haribo Ricqlès Zan. In 1996, Haribo opened the 'Musée du Bonbon' in Uzès, which gives a fascinating glimpse into the history of the production of liquorice, and bonbons.

Liquorice was a speciality of eighteenth-century Montpellier, capital of Languedoc-Roussillon, and was grown in the garrigues (scrubland). Apothecaries mixed liquorice with honey to produce small medicinal sweets called grisettes. These little round sweets coated with granulated (raw) sugar are still made in the town, sold in their distinctive yellow tins, and Grisettes de Montpellier are reputed to be the oldest sweet in France, originating in the twelfth century.

Montpellier has a tradition of sweet making that dates back centuries. In 1939, there were still six confiseries in Montepellier, but today there is only one company who produces traditional liquorice confectionery – Auzier Chabernac. Products such as liquorice pastilles, cachous and gums flavoured with vanilla, honey, mint or violet are the successors of those made by the apothecaries of long ago and remain popular today.

Cachou Lajaunie, tiny liquorice and mint sweets, were invented by pharmacist Léon Lajaunie in 1890 and are still made in Toulouse. Sold in the original small bright yellow tins (invented by a clock-maker friend of Lajaunie, who designed it to fit in a watch-pocket), they are a popular breath freshener in France.

France is home to well-known liquorice brands such as the little Grisettes of Montpellier, the tiny balls of liquorice coated in sugar and reputed to be one of the first French sweets; Cachou pastilles; and the varied products of the Zan company.

A history of liquorice in England

It's believed that liquorice was brought to Pontefract in West Yorkshire by Spanish monks in the Middle Ages, although its commercial cultivation began in about 1558, with a few plants also grown near London.

The rich sandy soil around Pontefract was found to be particularly suitable for cultivation – even though the English climate was too cold for the plants to flower, this was an advantage, as it made the liquorice roots even sweeter. English liquorice is best harvested after five years, unlike in Europe where it only takes three to four years to mature. The flavour of English liquorice was said to be superior to that of the Continental type, but liquorice growing was never practised in England on a very large scale.

By 1750, there were about forty-seven liquorice farmers in Pontefract. By 1840, liquorice cultivation had soared with hundreds of tons produced in the Pontefract area each week to supply Yorkshire's many large sweet manufacturers. During the Industrial Revolution more liquorice factories were established in the area, such as W. R. Wilkinson, who opened his Pontefract liquorice business in 1884. By 1900 seventeen factories were producing Pontefract Cakes. All the confectionery made in the local factories was originally produced by hand, and each factory had its own unique style. Liquorice production increased rapidly in the area in the 1940s with hundreds of tons produced for home use and also for export throughout the world.

At the start of World War II, Pontefract was producing four hundred tons of liquorice a week. After the war, production declined due to several factors but the practicalities of cultivation became increasingly uneconomical. It was a difficult plant to grow in England - the shrubs took considerably long to mature, the plants required a lot of care, and heavy rain and severe freezing could cause them to die. Unlike in their native countries where the plant behaves like a weed, liquorice rarely spreads naturally in England and must be grown from 'sets' (bud cuttings). The liquorice fields in and around Pontefract could not keep up with demand from the factories, and so confectionery companies started to import cheaper liquorice from Spain, before even less expensive supplies became available from Turkey, Iran and Iraq. Many Pontefract farmers gave up the crop altogether, replacing it with faster, easier cash crops, although some still kept a few plants in their gardens.

By the 1920s, only four liquorice growers remained in Pontefract and by the 1950s, there were only two. The last liquorice harvest in Pontefract took place in 1966 and today no commercial Pontefract liquorice growers remain. However, an enterprising Yorkshire farmer is now growing liquorice again in an attempt to re-establish its cultivation in the region.

The liquorice garths (fields) once so important to the town were commemorated by Sir John Betjeman in his 1953 poem, The Licorice Fields of Pontefract. Note his spelling!

'In the licorice fields at Pontefract
My love and I did meet
And many a burdened licorice bush
Was blooming round our feet'

The old Wilkinson liquorice factory; *the company still produces Pontefract Cakes – traditionally stamped by hand, though now machines are used. Liquorice was grown and harvested in local Pontefract fields for hundreds of years until the mid 1950s.*

Pontefract Cakes

The Priory of St. John the Evangelist stood on an area that we now know as Monkhill in Pontefract in West Yorkshire. Excavations revealed the remains of a medieval pharmacy where liquorice was extracted from the roots of the plant and used in the preparation of medicines. As far back as 1614, small liquorice lozenges were being produced to ease stomach disorders. A small stamp was applied to each round – an early form of what would become the famous Pontefract Cakes.

After the Dissolution of the Monasteries in the sixteenth century, Pontefract farmers continued to cultivate liquorice and a thriving cottage industry was established to process and refine the liquorice extract specifically for medicinal purposes. Families were contracted to supply liquorice and at harvest time all the family became involved, with the men digging up the roots and the women and children collecting them. They soaked the roots in hot water in their homes, crushed them through a mangle, then boiled the liquid on the kitchen cooking range.

In 1649, the town's castle was demolished and gardens established in its place, with liquorice among the plants cultivated in the gardens. In 1701 the Borough of Pontefract tried to ban the sale of liquorice plants outside the town in an attempt to prevent a rival industry being set up outside the Borough. Inhabitants of Pontefract were forbidden to sell, give or lend any liquorice shoots or buds to anyone outside the Borough and transgressors had to pay large fines, which were given to the poor.

In the eighteenth century, liquorice production was centered in Pontefract and its liquorice was sent all over the country. The Dunhill family leased land in the castle region in 1720 for the purpose of growing liquorice, and liquorice lovers can thank chemist George Dunhill for adding sugar to Pontefract Cakes in 1760 to make the first liquorice confectionery. He boiled raw liquorice, added sugar, molasses and flour and rolled the mixture into rounds, then sold it in his chemist's shop as a medicinal pastille for coughs and chest ailments. His customers also included miners on their way to work, as liquorice stopped them from being thirsty in the dusty coalmines.

Sweet 'Pontefract Cakes' proved enormously popular and farmers were contracted by confectionery makers to supply liquorice. By 1779 George Dunhill had established a thriving liquorice business. By the 1890s, liquorice was moving away from its medicinal origins and starting to be regarded as confectionery to be eaten for pleasure, although it remained an ingredient of throat and cough medicines and lozenges. Until the mid-twentieth century, the workers (usually women) were known as 'thumpers' or 'cakers' and were able to produce over 30,000 cakes per day. They rolled, cut and embossed Pontefract Cakes by hand. Machines replaced hand-making and stamping the cakes in the 1960s.

A Mr F. Craven took over the business in 1883, although the Dunhill name was kept and the business gradually expanded over the years to become a modern factory. In 1972 the German company Haribo acquired a major stake in Dunhills and in 1994 gained the remaining shares. The company continues to make the popular Pontefract Cakes under the Dunhill name using the original recipe and featuring the traditional stamp.

The distinctive stamp on the Pontefract Cakes features the castle of Pontefract; the original design also depicted an owl.

Liquorice Allsorts

Another notable name in English liquorice confectionery was George Bassett, who started his sweet company in 1842 in Sheffield. The company later bought their rival Wilkinson, in Pontefact, in 1961.

Allsorts are now made by different companies around the world, but the famous Bassett's Liquorice Allsorts were first created in 1899 when salesman Charlie Thompson dropped a tray of liquorice and sugarpaste samples. The individual items had been declined but when the customer saw the multicoloured mix together he was impressed, and placed the first order for 'allsorts'. The little sweets are made from combinations of liquorice, sugarpaste, coconut, aniseed jelly, fruit flavourings and gelatine, and each were given their own names – such as chips, rocks, buttons, cubes, nuggets, plugs, twists and spogs.

The company's well-known mascot Bertie Bassett (made up from a selection of different liquorice shapes) was created by John McEwan and launched in 1929. Bertie Bassett became hugely popular and the character was even made into cookie jars, mugs, soft toys, CD holders and moneyboxes, which are now sought-after by collectors of ephemera. To celebrate his 80th birthday on 12th February 2009, Bertie Bassett married his sweetheart Betty Bassett in the Bassett's factory in Sheffield where Allsorts are produced! Factory workers were given time off to celebrate with the happy couple.

The company created other popular sweets including the Sherbert Fountain, with a liquorice stick dipper. George Bassett and Co Ltd was bought by Cadbury-Shweppes in 1989; Bassett continued as a brand of Cadbury until it was bought by Mondelez International in 2010.

Allsorts are one of Bassett's signature sweets, with their distinctive combinations of shaped liquorice and sugarpaste. The popular Catherine wheels are long strips of liquorice wrapped around coloured 'spogs', which is the curious name for the little sugared aniseed jellies; traditionally only pink and blue spogs are in the mixed allsorts.

Liquorice confectionery around the world

*E*very nationality has its own particular favourite type of liquorice. In the UK, France, Australia and the USA a soft chewy confection made by mixing liquorice extract with sugar, water, gum and flour is the preferred choice. Conversely the Spanish and Italians prefer hard, intensely strong unsweetened liquorice confectionery made only from 100% pure liquorice extract, while the Dutch and Scandinavians have a passion for salty liquorice – the stronger and saltier the better!

Traditional British liquorice confectionery includes comfits and torpedoes (liquorice encased in a coloured hard-sugar shell), liquorice allsorts (black liquorice sandwiched in coloured sugarpaste, sometimes mint-flavoured), pipes, twists, wands, pinwheels and of course glossy, chewy Pontefract Cakes. Liquorice roots were sold in sweet shops throughout the UK in the 1950s and 60s, but are nowadays found in health shops.

In Italy unsweetened liquorice (liquirizia) is enjoyed in the form of sticks or small black pieces made from 100% pure liquorice extract, with a bitter and intense flavour. The latter are often sold in attractive little tins that are very collectable. Other popular types of liquorice include Telefone Cables – long, thin strips of sweet liquorice; Senatori alla Violetta – violet-flavoured liquorice pastilles; Sassolin – sugar-coated strong liquorice that look exactly like small pebbles; and berry-shaped chewy Morette all'arancia, which are flavoured with orange juice. In Spain, Italy and France liquorice root is chewed as a mouth freshener and digestive.

The Dutch are the world's largest consumers of liquorice and in the Netherlands, drop (liquorice) comes in many types and flavours. Drop Zoet is sweet liquorice and Drop Zout, the most popular, is salty liquorice. There are four main types of drop: soft and sweet, soft and salty, hard and sweet, and hard and salty, and it's often flavoured with mint, menthol or honey. Drop can be found anywhere, including pharmacies, as Dutch people also believe it has medicinal properties to treat sore throats and stomach aches.

Drop comes in many shapes and sizes from small Groente Erwten (green peas) to large Muntdrop (firm chewy coins). Shapes include rounds, squares, diamonds, ovals, cubes and novelty shapes such as cats (Katjes Drop) and cars (Autodrop). Zaanse Drops are soft and sweet; Griotten – a type of firm, dense marshmallow with a sugary crust – are light brown, chewy squares that look like sugar cubes. Rectangular-shaped Laurier Drops are firm and chewy; Schoolkrijt (school chalk) look like their description with a white minty outside shell and liquorice on the inside; Boerderij Drops are salty farm animals; Zakkenrollers (pickpockets) come shaped as tiny liquorice keys, mobile phones and watches; Paardenkoppen are horse heads; Oceaandrop are starfish, seahorse- and seashell-shaped candies covered in sea salt; and Scheepstouw (ship rope) are hard salty pieces that look like brown ropes.

The taste in most of the salty liquorice is due to ammonium chloride, a powder that tastes like salt, but isn't salt as we know it. The practice of adding it to liquorice is believed to have originated in pharmacies that prepared their own cough mixtures

A collection of typical British liquorice (top) with Catherine wheels, Pontefract cakes, allsorts, soft eating sticks, comfits and aniseed twists; other European products (bottom) include sticks dusted in cinnamon and sugar; liquorice shiny and hard, or soft and chewy...

A tempting range of classic liquorice from the Netherlands and Scandivania, where all kinds of sweet and salty shapes are popular, from herrings to skulls, pastilles, lozenges and the popular chocolate liquorice, as well as stacks of roots for infusing.

and pastilles; ammonium chloride was known for being able to break down mucus. The Latin term for ammonium chloride is sal ammoniac and salty liquorice is often called salmiakki. People began to buy the pastilles for enjoyment rather than medicinal purposes, and in the twentieth century, confectionery makers in Scandinavia and Holland started to make salmiak liquorice to satisfy demand – a trend that continues today.

As well as in the Netherlands, salty liquorice is very popular in Scandinavia, Northern Germany and Belgium. It's called salmiakk/saltlakris in Norwegian; saltlakrids in Danish; saltlakrits in Swedish; saltlakkrís in Icelandic; salzlakritze in German; and in Finland salty liquorice is usually called salmiakki, although this can also refer to other products containing ammonium chloride. In Dutch, the term dubbel zout (double salt) or salmiakdrop usually refers to salty liquorice with a high concentration of ammonium chloride. More ammonium chloride means stronger, saltier salmiakki. There's even triple-salted liquorice (seriously salty and not for the faint-hearted!) in these countries.

Salty liquorice is quite a shock to the palate if you're used to eating sweet liquorice. The sharp, sour, pungent flavour tingles on the tongue and takes some getting used to. Danish Heksehyl are a good choice for your first taste of salty liquorice as they're milder-flavoured soft, salty liquorice cylinders.

The Icelanders' favourite liquorice sweets are Opals – small sour liquorice lozenges that come in red (the most popular), green, black and pink varieties, which are hard at first but soften to become chewable. They're sold in attractive pop-art boxes designed by Atli Már Árnason. Other popular types include

Lakkrísrör (liquorice tube), which is commonly used as a straw for fizzy drinks, and black liquorice 'laces' filled with sweet yellow liquorice-flavoured cream or marzipan. Both chocolate and liquorice are Icelandic passions and the two are combined in many products, including Draumur (which means 'dream'), Icelandic milk chocolate with two liquorice strings inside; Lakkris Kulur (chocolate-covered marzipan with a liquorice centre); chocolate-covered black liquorice bars; and a chocolate bar filled with sweet, sticky liquorice that oozes out when bitten. Salty liquorice is popular in Northern Germany, but not in the southern part of Germany, where you are less likely to find liquorice products in the shops. Favourites include Salzige Heringe (salty herrings) – fish-shaped strongly salted liquorice; Salmiakdragees – crisp-coated dragees with a soft, slightly chewy salmiak liquorice centre in black, white, red, gold and silver colours; Sallos – spicy liquorice sweets with herbal extracts that soothe the throat; Sallos X-Presso – sweet liquorice caramels with liquid espresso in the centre; and Salmiak Creme Dreiecke Zartbitter – chocolate-covered triangles filled with salmiak fondant, a delicious combination of spice, salt and sweetness.

Another type of liquorice loved in Northern Europe is fiery Tyrkisk Peber (Turkish pepper). It goes by various names: Tyrkisk Peber in Denmark; Turkinpippuri in Finland; Tyrkisk Pepper in Norway; Turkisk Peppar in Sweden; and Türkisch Pfeffer in Germany. The strong liquorice is flavoured with ammonium chloride and pepper. They're strong and spicy sticks or hard-boiled sweets, with a generous amount of salmiak in the centres. In Northern Europe there are competing different versions of this sweet including Pulver Padder (that look like

toads), Rustne Søm, and Spejder-Hagl. In Iceland one of the most popular types are small liquorice balls, covered in milk chocolate and coated with hot pepper.

Tyrkisk Peber powder is sometimes used to make the Finnish cocktail salmiakkoskenkorva, and similar versions like the Danish sort svin, små grå, or hot shot; the Norwegian tyrker, små grå, or lakrisshot; and Swedish lakritsshot.

Although salty liquorice is hugely popular in Nordic countries, sweet liquorice is liked too. Danes love Trollen – strips of black liquorice wrapped around a chewy brown cream centre. In Sweden Bumlingar – round, hard balls of salty liquorice with a sweet salmiak flavour – are a favourite, as are Djúpur – little balls of slightly salty liquorice with a soft, mild salty liquorice centre combined with milk chocolate in a crisp sugar shell. Sterkar Djupur – salty liquorice covered in milk chocolate, with salmiak and liquorice powder – has no crisp coating, just a strong, peppery salmiak powder with a similar flavour to Turkish pepper.

A number of firm liquorice sweets are made with gum arabic (acacia gum), the resinous sap of some species of acacia tree, which is an excellent thickener, but it is also more expensive than wheat starch. However this type of liquorice has a cleaner, better-tasting flavour than cheaper liquorice, dissolves easily in the mouth and has no calories.

In the United States, anise (aniseed) extract is often used as a liquorice ('licorice' in the USA) flavouring, as it's less expensive. Although anise has a similar flavour to liquorice, due to its athenole content, the plant (Pimpinella anisum) is a member of the parsley family and is not related to liquorice. 'Black licorice' describes confectionery flavoured with licorice extract (sometimes also with anise), distinguishing it from similar products, made in the form of chewy ropes, twists or tubes. Red licorice is an enduring favourite, although it doesn't contain any liquorice extract; it is usually fruit-flavoured and the word 'licorice' is not present on the packaging. 'Red Vines', popular for decades in the USA, come in a variety of formats: single vines, pull-apart bars, textured bites, and chewy ropes or strings that are flavoured with strawberry, cherry, raspberry or cinnamon. Twizzlers, another American favourite, were originally made with liquorice but nowadays come in a variety of shapes, sizes and fruit flavours. The black versions are flavoured with liquorice extract, though this type is more popular in Europe.

The demand for high-quality liquorice is increasing all the time and new products are emerging to satisfy the growing demand for liquorice. There's now a huge choice – artisan handmade liquorice, organic, sugar-free, gluten-free, lactose-free and vegan, plus 'luxury' liquorice – chocolate-coated, chocolate bars, liquorice combined with other flavours such as chilli, fruit and caramel, and finely crushed salty liquorice which can be sprinkled over ice cream or cakes. This gourmet liquorice made with quality ingredients is a far cry from the low-priced sweetshop trays of the past.

Many forms of liquorice can be used in cooking – ground root powder, natural extract, dried roots, hard and soft sticks, and of course the confectionery itself: chewy sweets, wheels and the Pontefract Cakes can be melted, and used as decorations.

Liquorice festivals

Liquorice festivals are becoming increasingly popular throughout Europe and the USA. They're the perfect events for liquorice lovers to enjoy their favourite confectionery and to discover exciting new products - and indeed for anyone who would like to find out more about liquorice. These are just a few of the famous events to visit.

PONTEFRACT FESTIVAL

To celebrate the status of liquorice in the Pontefract area, a festival was created in the 1930s at a Christmas party at Wilkinson's factory dance, which held a dress competition with outfits made of liquorice. In 2004 Pontefract revived the Liquorice Festival with a fashion show where all the outfits and accessories were made of liquorice. Pontefract's now hugely successful annual liquorice festival attracts thousands of visitors and offers everything liquorice – including Pork & Liquorice Pies, Liquorice Stout, Liquorice Ice Cream and Pork & Liquorice Sausages. Keen gardeners can also buy liquorice plants.

LAKRITSFESTIVALEN

Stockholm's Liquorice Festival is the annual meeting place for liquorice lovers in Sweden. Here you can discover new liquorice favourites, enjoy a variety of tastings, take part in contests, experience liquorice-themed entertainment, cook liquorice dishes and enjoy a liquorice-based meal.

Liquorice festivals offer a chance to discover wonderful products old and new. The events offer stalls, fun displays and even organise culinary demonstrations, as at the Lakrids festival in Copenhagan.

LAKRIDSFESTIVAL

Copenhagen's Liquorice Festival in Denmark offers a fabulous selection of liquorice-based products including cakes, bread, chocolate and even beer. With tastings, recipes and tips on cooking, liquorice obsessives will love it!

LAKRITSI & SALMIAKKI FESTIVAALIT

Finland's celebration of 'black gold' in Helsinki every November features all types of liquorice and its use as a spice in cooking. Much is made of the famously salty salmiakki, flavoured with ammonium chloride, an acquired taste for many.

NATIONAL LICORICE DAY

Throughout the USA, National Licorice Day on April 12th (founded by Licorice International in 2014) celebrates every type of liquorice. The historic Haymarket District in Lincoln, Nebraska hosts lots of events to sing the praises of liquorice with more than one hundred and sixty types of liquorice from fourteen countries, and offering free samples, tastings, history and even workshops on making liquorice jewellery.

A cook's guide to liquorice

The unique flavour of liquorice makes it a brilliant cooking ingredient in both sweet and savoury dishes. It works particularly well with chocolate!

Liquorice roots, which look like hard woody twigs, exude their strong aroma without needing to be heated, for example by storing in a jar of sugar or salt. But they impart most flavour when steeped in hot liquid, such as teas, syrups, sauces, custards and in casseroles and stews, then removing before serving. You can change the intensity of flavour by using more or fewer roots or increasing the amount of time that the roots are steeped in the liquid.

Keep a couple of roots in a jar of sugar to make liquorice sugar, and use liquorice as a healthier substitute for sugar for sweetening foods, for example when stewing fruit. For savoury dishes, add one or two roots to a casserole or stew or add to stock for poaching meats.

Liquorice powder is made by steaming and pressing the roots and then grinding them into powder. It makes a useful addition to your spice cupboard. It dissolves easily and can be used as a seasoning; to flavour drinks such as milk or coffee; to add to barbecue rubs; and sprinkled on porridge, desserts, ice cream or sauces. Try mixing a little powdered liquorice into pasta dough: it's a great way of adding a little extra flavour to casseroles and stews. Pure liquorice granules are also available.

Sweet liquorice syrup is made from aniseed, cane sugar and liquorice. The delicate hint of fragrant aniseed makes a little syrup go a long way. Drizzle it over ice cream or fresh fruit or use in smoothies, desserts, marinades and cocktails. It makes a great glaze for poultry, on its own or mixed.

Salty liquorice syrup is made from cane sugar, ammonium chloride, liquorice and a touch of aniseed. It gives an unusual twist trickled over ice cream, desserts and fruits and can also be used for savoury marinades and glazes.

Hard liquorice has a more intense, slightly bitter flavour than the softer sticks usually sold in sweet shops. The hard form (sold in blocks, sticks and pellets) can be dissolved in liquid and used to impart both colour and liquorice flavour to recipes. It's best to use the hard shiny Italian liquorice, which is made from pure liquorice juice and has a strong bittersweet flavour.

Liquorice essence made from concentrated natural liquorice extract gives an intense liquorice flavour when added to cakes, icing, ice creams, chocolates, sweets and desserts. The strength varies according to the brand, but usually only a tiny amount is needed.

Anise is a pretty, white-flowered herb from which the tiny brown seeds (aniseed) and anise oil are obtained. The aromatic seeds and oil impart a distinctive, yet delicate liquorice taste. Anise is used in some liquorice recipes, both sweet and savoury, to complement and enhance the flavour and is also sometimes used in liqueurs.

Anise extract consists of alcohol, water and oil of anise and should be used sparingly. It imparts a subtle liquorice overtone to recipes, especially confectionery. The slightly sweet liquorice flavour is due to anethole, which is also found in fennel and tarragon.

Row by row, left to right: dried liquorice roots, and in caster sugar; powdered liquorice; liquorice syrup (available as sweet or salty); melting hard liquorice in a pan; pure liquorice sticks; natural liquorice colour essence; aniseeds; liquorice pinwheels or whirls.

Liquorice drinks

A non-alcoholic lemon-liquorice drink known as 'coco' was popular in Paris in the eighteenth and nineteenth centuries and was available from street vendors, dressed in white aprons and ringing a bell, who dispensed the drink from a metal canister on their backs into a tin cup. The name comes from the drink's milky white colour, which resembled coconut milk.

Sugarallie (liquorice water) was a popular drink, particularly in Scotland, in the nineteenth to mid-twentieth century. Children would make it by putting chopped black liquorice or liquorice root in a bottle of cold water and leaving it to stand for a week or so, shaking it from time to time. The name is a corruption of the sixteenth-century term 'sugar alicreesh' (black sugar or liquorice). Liquorice water is mentioned in some of Richmal Crompton's 'William' books, Charles Dickens' 'Great Expectations' and the Scottish cartoon 'Oor Wullie'. My late father had fond memories of enjoying the sweet black drink as a child in Tayport, Scotland. A popular rhyme of the time was 'Sugarallie water, as black as the lum (chimney), gather up pins, and I'll gie ye some' (a sip of liquorice water given in exchange for a pin, a button, etc.). It was a favourite drink with children as it was cheap and fun to make.

Liquorice liqueurs are much in demand, such as Antica Sambuca (Black) Liquorice Liqueur; Calabrian Tosolini Luna Nera (Black Moon) Liquorice Liqueur and Grappa Liquirizia from Italy; the French pastis and liquorice-flavoured absinthe;

Finland's Koskenkorva Salmiakki, vodka made with salty liquorice; Znaps, Black Jack Liquorice Shooter and thick black Pistonhead Crude Oil Liquorice Chilli Liqueur from Sweden; and Iceland's spicy Fjallagrasa Svartur Soprano Schnapps. In the UK there's a range of liquorice-flavoured beers and English liquorice gin. Blackcurrant and liquorice cordial, an old fashioned non-alcoholic English drink, is still popular today.

A long-standing favourite in Egypt and Syria, the refreshing non-alcoholic liquorice drink erk sous is sold in shops and by street vendors in the markets. The vendors carry an ice-filled copper container and pour the drink into a glass or cup for the customer.

The simplest drink can be the best: make a cup of liquorice tea to sip after a meal to aid digestion by infusing ½–1 teaspoon of chopped root in a cup of boiling water and leave to brew to your liking; you can vary the flavour by adding a slice or two of root ginger or lemon.

Refreshing liquorice tea: just add boiling water to shards of root and allow to steep, or make it with cold water. There is a reason this simple drink has been popular for centuries in North Africa, it is a wonderful thirst-quencher and restorative.

Savoury dishes

Liquorice is a versatile ingredient that imparts an unusual and intriguing depth of flavour to many savoury dishes, especially when combined with other spices. Take inspiration from Morocco, India and the Far East where liquorice has long been used in spice blends, marinades and sauces, and adds subtle interest to your salads, risottos, meat and fish cooking.

Liquorice makes an unusual dressing and is sure to become a talking point with guests. Serve this distinctive tasting salad on its own or as an accompaniment to cold meats, poultry and game or rich, oily fish such as mackerel – the refreshing citrus flavours cut through the richness of the meat or fish.

Citrus fruit salad with liquorice vinaigrette

SERVES 4–5

Salty liquorice syrup adds a sharp taste to this dressing

15ml/1 tbsp salty liquorice syrup
30ml/2 tbsp dark balsamic vinegar
2 oranges, peeled, pith removed, thinly sliced
1 blood orange, peeled, pith removed, thinly sliced
2 ruby grapefruit, peeled, pith removed, thinly sliced
1 plain grapefruit, peeled, pith removed, thinly sliced
1 small red onion, very thinly sliced
1 avocado, peeled and sliced thinly

TO GARNISH
Mint sprigs

1 Whisk together the liquorice syrup and vinegar until well combined. Set aside.

2 Arrange the fruit slices on a serving plate and add the onion and avocado slices.

3 Drizzle with the dressing and garnish with mint.

Energy 111kcal/467kJ; Protein 2.3g; Carbohydrate 17.3g, of which sugars 16.1g; Fat 4.1g, of which saturates 0.8g; Cholesterol 0mg; Calcium 67mg; Fibre 4.8g; Sodium 9mg.

A deliciously creamy risotto with the unexpected flavour of liquorice. Liquorice root is finely ground into a powder and used like a spice. It has a deep flavour and natural sweetness that makes it perfect for both savoury and sweet dishes.

Liquorice & pine nut risotto

SERVES 4

55g/2oz/¼ cup butter
1 onion, finely chopped
1 clove garlic, crushed
300g/11oz/1½ cups
    Arborio rice
120ml/4fl oz/½ cup white wine
1 litre/1¾ pints/4 cups hot
    vegetable stock
Salt and pepper
2.5–5ml/½–1 tsp powdered
    liquorice, plus extra for dusting
45–60ml/3–4 tbsp pine nuts,
    toasted

TO GARNISH
Grated Parmesan cheese

1 Heat half the butter in a large pan and cook the onion and garlic over a low heat until softened and transparent.

2 Add the rice and stir to coat all the grains. Increase the heat and add the wine. Cook until absorbed.

3 Gradually add the stock, a ladleful at a time, stirring until absorbed, before adding more stock. Continue cooking until the rice is tender, but still has a little bite. Season to taste with salt and pepper.

4 Stir in the liquorice powder and the remaining butter. Put into warm serving bowls and sprinkle with a little extra liquorice powder and the pine nuts. Garnish with grated Parmesan cheese.

Energy 476kcal/1979kJ; Protein 7.5g; Carbohydrate 62.2g, of which sugars 1.8g; Fat 19.5g, of which saturates 7.7g; Cholesterol 29mg; Calcium 29mg; Fibre 0.7g; Sodium 85mg.

Aromatic liquorice and fennel are an excellent contrast to the subtle-tasting trout. Fennel seeds have a slight liquorice flavour already and complement the powdered liquorice in this easy recipe. Serve hot or cold for a lunch or light meal.

Liquorice & fennel trout fillets

SERVES 4

4 trout fillets
15ml/1 tbsp powdered liquorice
5ml/1 tsp sea salt
75ml/5 tbsp finely chopped walnuts
25ml/1½ tbsp fennel seeds
20ml/4 tsp sunflower oil

TO SERVE
Green vegetables, such as samphire (pictured), green beans or mangetouts (snow peas)

TO GARNISH
Lemon wedges

1 Heat the oven to 200°C/180°C fan/400°F/Gas 6. Grease a baking dish or sheet.

2 Put the trout, skin side down, on the baking sheet.

3 Mix together all the other ingredients in a bowl and press on to the trout.

4 Bake for 12–15 minutes, until the fish flakes easily with a fork and the topping is lightly browned.

5 Serve with vegetables and garnish with lemon wedges.

Energy 305kcal/1267kJ; Protein 28.2g; Carbohydrate 0.6g, of which sugars 0.5g; Fat 22.6g, of which saturates 1.9g; Cholesterol 0mg; Calcium 126mg; Fibre 0.9g; Sodium 568mg.

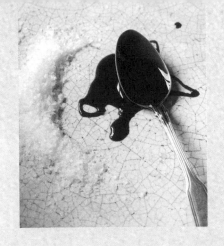

The subtle undertones of liquorice powder and syrup, and a touch of anise from the fennel seeds, really lifts this baked chicken and stimulates the tastebuds. You can use salty liquorice syrup instead of sweet – it's a matter of personal preference. If you opt for salty syrup, omit the salt from the rub mixture.

Liquorice glazed chicken

SERVES 4

4 chicken joints, skin on, bone in
20ml/4 tsp powdered liquorice
10ml/2 tsp paprika
5ml/1 tsp fennel seeds, crushed
Salt and pepper
20ml/4 tsp vegetable oil
20ml/4 tsp sweet liquorice
   syrup

TO SERVE
Crisp green salad
Lemon wedges

1 Make cuts in the chicken joints with a sharp knife through the skin.

2 Mix together the powdered liquorice, paprika, fennel, salt and pepper and rub into the chicken joints. Leave to stand for 1 hour.

3 Preheat the oven to 200°C/180°C fan/400°F/Gas 6.

4 Place the chicken in a baking dish and drizzle with the oil, followed by the liquorice syrup.

5 Cook for 20–30 minutes, until the chicken is cooked through, with no pink juices when pierced with a skewer.

6 Serve with a crisp green salad and lemon wedges, squeezing the wedges over the chicken.

Energy 325kcal/1352kJ; Protein 31.2g; Carbohydrate 3.9g, of which sugars 2.8g; Fat 21.1g, of which saturates 6.2g; Cholesterol 138mg; Calcium 57mg; Fibre 0g; Sodium 118mg.

This stylish dish would be great for a dinner party. The liquorice glaze adds an intriguing flavour. You can use partridge, grouse or chicken breasts instead of pheasant and adjust the cooking time accordingly. If you want even more of a liquorice hit you could add one or two star anise with the stock and remove them at the same time as the liquorice roots. This is delicious served with braised red cabbage and roast potatoes.

Pheasant with liquorice glaze

SERVES 4

4 pheasant breasts
Salt and ground black pepper
15ml/1 tbsp vegetable oil
15ml/1 tbsp butter
500ml/17fl oz/generous 2 cups
  stock
125ml/4fl oz/½ cup dry sherry
25ml/1½ tbsp redcurrant jelly
3 liquorice roots, crushed
15ml/1 tbsp sherry vinegar

TO SERVE
Braised red cabbage

1 Season the pheasant breasts with a little salt and pepper.

2 Heat a frying pan until medium-hot, add the oil and butter and fry the pheasant breasts, flesh side down, for 3–4 minutes until golden-brown.

3 Turn the breasts over, increase the heat and fry for a further 4–6 minutes, until the skin is golden-brown and crisp and the breasts are medium-rare. Remove from the heat and set the breasts aside to rest for a few minutes.

4 Add the stock, sherry, redcurrant jelly and liquorice to the pan. Bring to the boil, stirring to dissolve the redcurrant jelly and dislodge any sediment.

5 Boil steadily until thickened and reduced by about half. Strain into a small pan, discarding the liquorice. Add sherry vinegar to taste and season with salt and pepper.

6 Place the pheasant on warm serving plates and pour over the liquorice glaze. Serve immediately.

Energy 269kcal/1119kJ; Protein 21g; Carbohydrate 4.5g, of which sugars 4.5g; Fat 14.8g, of which saturates 5.4g; Cholesterol 173mg; Calcium 24mg; Fibre 0g; Sodium 76mg.

The mellow taste of liquorice complements pork and adds a subtle burst of unexpected flavour to a traditional roast. Liquorice powder works really well in both savoury and sweet dishes. I used powdered liquorice from Calabria to make this recipe, it has a very strong intense bittersweetness and is frequently used in the region's cuisine. Serve with roasted vegetables.

Liquorice roast pork

SERVES 4–6

1.5kg/3⅓lb boneless pork roasting joint (or 2kg/4½lb with bone)
10–15ml/2–3 tsp vegetable oil
10ml/2 tsp salt
15ml/1 tbsp powdered liquorice
1 clove garlic, crushed

TO SERVE
Roast vegetables, such as potatoes, red onions, garlic
  and sweet red (bell) peppers

1 Preheat the oven to 200°C/180°C fan/400°F/Gas 6.

2 Score the pork rind deeply with a sharp knife. Brush the rind with a little oil.

3 Mix together the salt, liquorice and garlic and rub well into the rind.

4 Place the meat in a roasting pan and cook for 30 minutes.

5 Reduce the oven temperature to 180°C/160°C fan/350°F/ Gas 4 and cook for a further 1¾ hours, until the pork is cooked and the rind is crisp. Allow the pork to rest for 15 minutes before carving.

Energy 324kcal/1365kJ; Protein 54.5g; Carbohydrate 0g, of which sugars 0g; Fat 11.8g, of which saturates 3.7g; Cholesterol 158mg; Calcium 18mg; Fibre 0g; Sodium 813mg.

The combination of treacle, orange and spices in the cooking liquor includes the slightly liquorice-tasting star anise, which together result in wonderfully tasty ham. It's ideal for serving cold at a buffet or special occasion lunch and makes fabulous sandwiches in dark rye bread with crisp green salad leaves. Serve it as it is, or with chutney.

Liquorice & orange glazed ham

SERVES 4–5

2kg/4½lb piece boneless gammon
Orange juice
8 liquorice roots, crushed
2 unwaxed oranges, cut in half
2 bay leaves
3 star anise
6 cloves
30ml/2 tbsp black treacle

TO GARNISH
Halved oranges
Bay leaves

1 Place the gammon into a large, deep pan and cover with water. Bring to the boil, then remove from the heat and drain.

2 Pour in enough orange juice to cover half of the gammon, then top up with enough cold water to cover the gammon completely. Add the remaining ingredients and bring to the boil.

3 Reduce the heat, cover and simmer for 20 minutes per 500g/ 1¼lb. Remove from the heat and leave to cool for 1 hour.

4 Strain the cooking liquid into a clean pan and bring to the boil. Cook steadily until reduced to a syrup.

5 Preheat the oven to 200°C/180° fan/400°F/Gas 6. Carefully remove the skin from the ham, leaving a layer of fat. Put into a roasting pan and score the fat in a diamond pattern with a sharp knife. Brush the ham all over with some of the syrup, then put in the oven for about 20 minutes until the glaze is bubbling. Brush on more glaze halfway through cooking.

6 Allow the ham to stand for 20 minutes. Garnish with halved oranges and bay leaves. Wrap the cold ham and store in the refrigerator for up to 3 days or freeze (well wrapped) for up to 1 month.

Energy 585kcal/2440kJ; Protein 70.2g; Carbohydrate 8.5g, of which sugars 8.4g; Fat 30g, of which saturates 10g; Cholesterol 92mg; Calcium 85mg; Fibre 0g; Sodium 3540mg.

Liquorice pairs well with pork in these succulent patties. They're delicious in a bread roll or served on a bed of crisp leaves with potato salad, coleslaw or pickles. They're also great for a barbecue – just brush the patties with a little oil and cook on the grill. You can substitute beef or venison for the pork.

Pork & liquorice patties

Serve the patties in a toasted bun with a green salad.

SERVES 4–6

400g/14oz minced (ground) pork
1 onion, grated
2 cloves garlic, crushed
Salt and pepper
45ml/3 tbsp fresh breadcrumbs
15ml/1 tbsp powdered liquorice
1 egg yolk, beaten
45ml/3 tbsp vegetable oil

TO SERVE
Burger or brioche bun, salad, red onions, coleslaw and condiments

1 Mix together the meat, onion, garlic, salt, pepper, breadcrumbs, liquorice and egg yolk and leave to stand for 20 minutes. Form into 4–6 patties.

2 Heat the oil in a frying pan and fry the patties for 3–4 minutes on each side, until golden brown and cooked through. Serve immediately.

Energy 203kcal/848kJ; Protein 14.6g; Carbohydrate 7.5g, of which sugars 1.4g; Fat 13.1g, of which saturates 3.3g; Cholesterol 78mg; Calcium 38mg; Fibre 0.6g; Sodium 103mg.

Desserts & puddings

The bold taste of liquorice makes the most delectable cakes, puddings, desserts and ice creams. It has a natural affinity with chocolate, as we know from the Danish confectionery – the combination is a match made in heaven if you love both liquorice and chocolate.

A dark, not too sweet, intensely flavoured ice cream. It's not essential to add black food colouring, but it does give a dramatic touch! It can be scooped into cones or served with a dessert, such as liquorice syrup and orange puddings; pear, liquorice and almond crumble; or spiced apple and raisin pie – the recipes are in this book.

Liquorice ice cream

SERVES 6–8

100g/3½oz hard black
 liquorice, chopped
200ml/7fl oz/scant 1 cup water
200ml/7fl oz/scant 1 cup milk
300ml/10fl oz/1¼ cups
 double (heavy) cream
Seeds from ½ vanilla pod (bean)
4 large egg yolks
50g/2oz/¼ cup caster
 (superfine) sugar
Black food colouring paste
 or gel, optional

TO SERVE
Ice cream cones

1 Put the liquorice and water in a pan and bring to the boil. Reduce the heat and simmer very gently, stirring frequently, for 15 minutes, until the liquorice has largely melted and you have a dark syrup. Remove from the heat.

2 In another pan, heat the milk, cream and vanilla seeds to just below boiling, then cover and set aside to infuse.

3 Whisk together the egg yolks and sugar in a large bowl. Whisk in the hot cream, then return to the pan and cook over a gentle heat, stirring all the time, until the custard has thickened. Do not boil or the mixture will curdle.

4 Pour into the melted liquorice, and add the colouring if using. Stir, then pour through a sieve or strainer into a jug. Place a piece of clear film or plastic wrap directly on to the surface of the custard, to stop a skin forming. Leave to cool, then chill.

5 Churn in an ice cream machine according to the manufacturer's instructions. Cover and freeze for 2–3 hours until firm. If making without a machine, pour into a freezerproof container and freeze for 4–5 hours, beating with a fork every hour during freezing, to break up the ice crystals. Eat within 2 weeks.

Energy 287kcal/1193kJ; Protein 3.6g; Carbohydrate 16.5g, of which sugars 13.6g; Fat 23.5g, of which saturates 13.6g; Cholesterol 154mg; Calcium 114mg; Fibre 0.3g; Sodium 49mg.

A different take on traditional cheesecake, this irresistible version with a buttery base and velvety creamy topping is a wow with liquorice lovers. It has a deep, rich treacly flavour and is delicious on its own or served with raspberries or strawberries.

Liquorice cheesecake

SERVES 4–6

FOR THE BASE
200g/7oz shortbread biscuits (cookies), crushed to crumbs
100g/3½oz/scant ½ cup butter, melted

FOR THE TOPPING
600g/1lb 5oz/2½ cups full fat cream cheese
30ml/2 tbsp lemon juice
100g/3½oz/scant ½ cup caster (superfine) sugar
30–45ml/2–3 tbsp powdered liquorice
45ml/3 heaped tbsp black treacle (molasses)
200ml/7oz/scant 1 cup double (heavy) cream
Liquorice wheels or bootlaces

1 Butter a 20cm/8in springform tin or pan.

2 Stir together the shortbread crumbs and melted butter. Press firmly into the base of the tin and chill for at least 30 minutes.

3 Beat together the cream cheese, lemon juice and sugar.

4 Beat in the liquorice and treacle until smooth.

5 Whisk the cream until very thick and standing in peaks, and gently stir into the cream cheese mixture until well blended. Spoon the mixture over the biscuit base.

6 Decorate with the liquorice wheels or bootlaces, chopped to make a pattern of your choice.

7 Cover and chill for at least 3 hours until firm enough to slice. Cover and store in the refrigerator for up to 4 days or wrap well in foil and freeze for up to 2 months.

Energy 983kcal/4071kJ; Protein 6.4g; Carbohydrate 44.2g, of which sugars 28.3g; Fat 88.3g, of which saturates 55.6g; Cholesterol 201mg; Calcium 237mg; Fibre 0g; Sodium 513mg.

A twist on the classic dessert, with a rich and creamy black liquorice custard and crisp sugar topping. As a variation you could sprinkle a few berries (blueberries or blackberries are good) in the buttered ramekins before topping with the custard mixture. Use cane sugar for the topping, not beet sugar, which inclines to burn. For the best results, spread the sugar on a plate and put it in a low oven for a few minutes to dry out. This bruleé has an intensive liquorice flavour – if you would prefer a less powerful taste, reduce the amount of liquorice to 75g/3oz.

Liquorice crème brûlée

SERVES 4–6

450ml/14fl oz/2 cups double (heavy) cream
110g/4oz hard black liquorice, chopped
55g/2oz/¼ cup cane sugar
1 pinch salt
3 egg yolks
5ml/1 tsp vanilla extract

FOR SPRINKLING
60–90ml/4–6 tbsp sugar

1 Preheat the oven to 150°C/130°C fan/300°F/Gas 2. Butter 4–6 ramekins.

2 Combine half the cream with the liquorice in a pan. Heat over a medium heat until the liquorice has melted. Remove from the heat and add the remaining cream.

3 Add the sugar and salt to the pan and stir over a medium heat until the sugar has dissolved.

4 Beat together the egg yolks and vanilla until smooth in a heatproof bowl. Pour the hot liquorice cream into the yolks, a little at a time, stirring constantly, until blended. Strain the mixture into the ramekins.

5 Place the ramekins in a roasting pan or large baking dish and add enough hot water to come halfway up. Cover with foil and bake for 25–30 minutes, until the custards have just set. Leave to cool, then chill for at least 2 hours.

6 Heat the grill or broiler until very hot. Sprinkle the custards with sugar and put under the grill until the sugar bubbles and caramelises. Alternatively, caramelise the sugar with a chef's blowtorch. Serve within 2 hours or the caramel will melt.

Energy 142kcal/600kJ; Protein 2.6g; Carbohydrate 21.6g, of which sugars 17.3g; Fat 5.7g, of which saturates 2.5g; Cholesterol 108mg; Calcium 98mg; Fibre 0.5g; Sodium 41mg.

Black and white marbled meringues look impressive and taste divine served with a scoop of whipped cream or ice cream and perhaps a few dark berries (blackcurrants, blackberries or blueberries) to tone with the colour of the meringues.

Liquorice meringues

MAKES 10

2 egg whites
Pinch of salt
100g/3½oz/scant ½ cup
   caster (superfine) sugar
10ml/2 tsp powdered liquorice
1.5ml/¼ tsp black food
   colouring gel or paste

1 Preheat the oven to its lowest setting. Line 2 large baking sheets with baking parchment.

2 Whisk the egg whites and salt with an electric whisk until beginning to form peaks.

3 Gradually whisk in the caster sugar until thick and shiny. Gently fold in the liquorice powder.

4 Add the food colouring and using a skewer, cocktail stick or toothpick, swirl through the meringue mixture to get a marbled effect.

5 Spoon about 10 rounds on to the baking sheets.

6 Bake for 1 hour–1 hour 15 minutes, until the meringues sound crisp when tapped underneath. Turn the oven off and leave to cool in the oven for a further hour. Place on a wire rack to cool completely. Store in an airtight container for up to 2 days.

Energy 42kcal/178kJ; Protein 0.7g; Carbohydrate 10.5g, of which sugars 10.5g; Fat 0g, of which saturates 0g; Cholesterol 0mg; Calcium 9mg; Fibre 0g; Sodium 13mg.

A variation of the classic nostalgic steamed syrup pudding and the perfect cold weather comfort food. When the hot puddings are turned out, the liquorice syrup flows over the top. You can omit the candied orange peel if you wish, but it does add a little extra to the flavour. Serve with whipped cream or pouring cream or with a scoop of delectable liquorice ice cream.

Liquorice syrup & orange puddings

SERVES 6

75–90ml/5–6 tbsp sweet
  liquorice syrup
30ml/2 tbsp candied orange
  peel, thinly sliced
150g/5oz/1¼ cup butter
150g/5oz/1¼ cup caster
  (superfine) sugar
3 eggs, beaten
150g/5oz/1¼ cups self-raising
  (self-rising) flour

1 Butter 6 x 125ml/4fl oz pudding basins or heatproof bowls and spoon the liquorice syrup and candied peel strips over the bases.

2 Beat the butter and sugar in a mixing bowl until light, then beat in the eggs until smooth.

3 Stir in the flour and mix well until blended.

4 Spoon into the basins and smooth the tops. Cover with a lid or a double thickness of pleated baking parchment, then with a double thickness of pleated foil (to allow for expansion as the pudding cooks).

5 Tie securely and place on a trivet or upturned plate in a large pan. Pour in boiling water to come halfway up the basins. Cover the pan and boil gently for 40 minutes. Cool in the basins for a few minutes then turn out on to warm serving plates.

6 If you prefer to make in one large basin, use a 1 litre/1¾ pint pudding bowl and steam for about 1½ hours.

Energy 461kcal/1931kJ; Protein 6.3g; Carbohydrate 58.1g, of which sugars 36.6g; Fat 24.3g, of which saturates 14g; Cholesterol 169mg; Calcium 118mg; Fibre 1.4g; Sodium 299mg.

Pears make a nice change from the usual apple in this satisfying pudding topped with liquorice-flavoured crumble, although of course you can use apples instead of pears if you wish. Instead of almonds you could use hazelnuts or pecans to add that little bit of extra crunch.

Pear, liquorice & almond crumble

SERVES 4

FOR THE FILLING
6 large pears, peeled, cored and chopped into chunks
30–50g/1–2oz/⅛–¼ cup granulated (white) sugar
15ml/1 tbsp plain (all-purpose) flour
Pinch of ground mixed (apple pie) spice

FOR THE CRUMBLE
175g/6oz/1½ cups plain (all-purpose) flour
85g/3oz/⅓ cup chilled butter, plus extra for greasing
85g/3oz/⅓ cup granulated (white) sugar
15ml/1 tbsp powdered liquorice
75g/3oz/1 cup flaked (sliced) almonds

1 Preheat the oven to 180°C/160°C fan/350°F/Gas 4. Butter a large baking dish.

2 Mix together the pears, sugar, flour and spice and place the mixture in the baking dish.

3 For the crumble, put the flour in a mixing bowl. Rub the butter into the flour until the mixture resembles fine breadcrumbs, and then stir in the sugar and liquorice.

4 Sprinkle evenly over the fruit and scatter over the almonds. Bake for about 30 minutes until golden brown. Eat immediately or cover when cold and store in the refrigerator for up to 3 days.

The pudding can be prepared ahead of time and makes a great family dessert.

Energy 698kcal/2931kJ; Protein 10.1g; Carbohydrate 105.9g, of which sugars 69.2g; Fat 29g, of which saturates 12g; Cholesterol 45mg; Calcium 187mg; Fibre 13g; Sodium 146mg.

There's nothing to beat a home-made apple pie and this all-time classic treat is given a makeover with five spice powder and liquorice. Five spice powder is a mixture of star anise, cinnamon, fennel, cloves, nutmeg, Sichuan pepper and ginger and adds an intriguing flavour. You can use dried cranberries or sultanas instead of raisins. The pie is delicious served warm or cold with whipped cream or ice cream.

Spiced apple & raisin pie

SERVES 6

FOR THE PASTRY
350g/12oz/3 cups plain
  (all-purpose) flour
Pinch of salt
175g/6oz/¾ cup butter
60–75ml/4–5 tbsp water, plus
  extra for brushing

FOR THE FILLING
900g/2lb cooking apples,
  peeled, cored and sliced
80g/3oz/⅓ cup soft light brown
  sugar
15ml/1 tbsp plain (all-purpose)
  flour
70g/2½oz/½ cup raisins
10ml/2 tsp powdered liquorice
2.5ml/½ tsp five spice powder

TO DECORATE
Icing (confectioners') sugar

1 For the pastry, sift the flour into a mixing bowl and stir in the salt. Rub in the butter until the mixture resembles breadcrumbs. Gradually add the water, until the mixture just comes together. If it is too stiff add a little more water. Roll the dough into a ball, then wrap in clear film or plastic wrap and chill for 30 minutes.

2 Preheat the oven to 200°C/180°C fan/400°F/Gas 6. Grease a deep 23cm/9in pie or flan dish. Mix all the filling ingredients together in a bowl until well combined.

3 Roll out just over half the pastry on a floured surface and line the dish, leaving an overhang of 1cm/½in around the edge of the dish. Spoon in the filling.

4 Roll out the remaining pastry to cover the pie and lightly brush the edges with a little water. Place over the filling, pressing the edges to seal. Make a hole in the centre of the pie to allow the steam to escape.

5 Bake for 30 minutes until golden, then reduce the oven temperature to 180°C/160°C fan/350°F/Gas 4 and bake for a further 15 minutes, until the pastry is golden and the apples are soft. Cool and dust with icing sugar before serving.

Energy 561kcal/2360kJ; Protein 6.8g; Carbohydrate 82.8g, of which sugars 36.5g; Fat 25g, of which saturates 15.3g; Cholesterol 62mg; Calcium 115mg; Fibre 6g; Sodium 189mg.

Cookies, cupcakes & baking

Using liquorice in baking cakes, cookies and bread adds another dimension to the flavour, which can be enhanced by using liquorice in the icings and frostings too. Adjust the amount of liquorice to your personal taste. You can also use one or two dried liquorice roots, in the same way as vanilla pods, to flavour a jar of sugar.

Black food colouring and black liquorice add a twist to classic red velvet cupcakes – perfect as a Halloween treat! The black liquorice may not melt completely but this is fine. If you can get it, use hard black Italian liquorice for the best flavour. The treacle and dark brown sugar in the buttercream add a dark depth to supplement the liquorice in the cakes.

Black velvet cupcakes

MAKES 12

120g/4½oz black liquorice, chopped
110g/4oz/½ cup butter
2 eggs
75g/3oz/⅓ cup caster (superfine) sugar
110g/4oz/1 cup self-raising (self-rising) flour
5ml/1 tsp baking powder
Few drops black food colouring

FOR THE BUTTERCREAM:
15ml/1 tbsp treacle (molasses)
100g/4oz/½ scant cup unsalted butter
50g/2oz/¼ cup dark muscovado (molasses) sugar
200g/8oz/1 cup cream cheese

1 Preheat the oven 170°C/150°C fan/325°F/Gas 3. Place 12 paper cases in deep bun tins or pans.

2 Put the liquorice and 75ml/5 tbsp water in a small pan over a low heat until the liquorice has almost melted. Add the butter and stir until melted. Put to one side.

3 Whisk together the eggs and sugar in a mixing bowl until doubled in volume and pale in colour.

4 Add the liquorice mixture and beat well until blended.

5 Sift over the flour and baking powder and beat again. Stir in the food colouring.

6 Spoon into the paper cases, filling three-quarters full. Bake for about 20 minutes until risen and springy to the touch. Cool in the tin for 5 minutes then place on a wire rack to cool completely.

7 To make the buttercream, beat together all the ingredients until well mixed. Chill until thick and pipeable.

8 Spoon into a piping bag and pipe a swirl on each cake. Serve the same day or store them in the refrigerator overnight.

Energy 319kcal/1332kJ; Protein 3.3g; Carbohydrate 25.3g, of which sugars 16g; Fat 23.4g, of which saturates 14.3g; Cholesterol 92mg; Calcium 113mg; Fibre 0.6g; Sodium 214mg.

These liquorice-flavoured cupcakes topped with creamy liquorice buttercream conceal a surprise in the centre. These are always a hit with children (who like liquorice!) as they bite into the hidden centre and are also popular at fêtes and fundraising events.

Surprise liquorice allsorts cupcakes

MAKES 12

200ml/7fl oz/scant 1 cup milk
2 star anise
115g/4oz/½ cup butter
150g/5oz/⅔ cup caster
   (superfine) sugar
2 eggs, beaten
175g/6oz/1½ cups self-raising
   (self-rising) flour
2.5ml/½ tsp baking powder
6 liquorice allsorts, halved
   and chilled

FOR THE BUTTERCREAM
150g/5oz/⅔ cup butter
500g/1lb 2oz/5 cups icing
   (confectioners') sugar
50ml/2fl oz/¼ cup milk
2.5–5ml/½–1 tsp natural
   liquorice essence

1 Heat the milk and star anise in a pan and bring just to the boil. Remove from the heat, cover and leave to infuse for about 30 minutes.

2 Preheat the oven to 180°C/160°C fan/350°F/Gas 4. Place 12 paper cases in deep bun tins or pans.

3 Beat the butter and sugar in a mixing bowl until light and creamy.

4 Beat in the eggs until blended. Sift in the flour and baking powder and gently fold into the mixture with the milk (discard the star anise), until well combined.

5 Spoon a little mixture into the paper cases and top with a liquorice allsort half. Cover completely with mixture and bake for 20–25 minutes until golden and springy to the touch. Cool in the tins for 5 minutes, then place on a wire rack to cool completely.

6 For the buttercream, beat the butter until soft, then gradually beat in the icing sugar with an electric whisk until the texture is sandy, then add the milk and liquorice essence. Whisk until light and fluffy.

7 Spoon into a piping bag and pipe a decorative pattern on each cake. Serve the same day or store them in the refrigerator overnight.

Energy 408kcal/1713kJ; Protein 2.2g; Carbohydrate 59.2g, of which sugars 58.5g; Fat 19.7g, of which saturates 12.1g; Cholesterol 87mg; Calcium 40mg; Fibre 0g; Sodium 165mg.

Liquorice and chocolate are a match made in heaven. Adults and children love these delicious muffins, which can be made with plain, milk or white chocolate chips. The liquorice buttercream makes them extra special. Brands of liquorice essence vary in strength, so add sparingly at first and taste as you go.

Chocolate chip muffins with liquorice buttercream

MAKES 12

175g/6oz/¾ cup butter
175g/6oz/¾ cup caster
  (superfine) sugar
2 eggs, beaten
45–60ml/3–4 tbsp milk
175g/6oz/1½ cups plain
  (all-purpose) flour
5ml/1 tsp baking powder
Pinch of salt
75g/3oz/½ cup plain
  (semisweet) chocolate,
  chopped small, or chocolate
  chips

FOR THE BUTTERCREAM
150g/5oz/⅔ cup unsalted
  butter
500g/1lb 2oz/5 cups icing
  (confectioners') sugar
50ml/2fl oz/¼ cup single
  (light) cream
2.5–5ml/½–1 tsp natural
  liquorice essence

TO DECORATE
1 small bar of milk chocolate,
  for grating

1 Preheat the oven to 180°C/160°C fan/350°F/Gas 4. Place 12 paper cases in a muffin tin or pan.

2 Beat the butter and both sugars in a mixing bowl until light and fluffy.

3 Gradually beat in the eggs and milk, beating until fully incorporated into the mixture.

4 Sift in the dry ingredients and gently stir into the mixture. Fold in the chocolate.

5 Spoon into the paper cases. Bake for about 20 minutes, until golden and risen. Cool in the tin for 5 minutes then place on a wire rack to cool completely.

6 For the liquorice buttercream, beat the butter and icing sugar with an electric whisk, then add the cream and liquorice essence. Whisk until light and fluffy.

7 Spoon into a piping bag and pipe a swirl on each muffin. Finely grate the milk chocolate over the top and serve immediately or store in the refrigerator overnight.

Energy 527kcal/2218kJ; Protein 3.5g; Carbohydrate 74.4g, of which sugars 62.7g; Fat 25.9g, of which saturates 15.9g; Cholesterol 100mg; Calcium 59mg; Fibre 0.7g; Sodium 157mg.

Chocolate and liquorice is a delicious combination and these delectable brownies with their deep intense flavour make an extra special treat. Be careful not to overbake the brownies or you'll lose the famous fudgy brownie texture – they should be slightly soft in the middle.

Liquorice brownies

MAKES 12–16

225g/8oz plain (semisweet)
  chocolate, 70% cocoa solids
150g/5oz/⅔ cup butter
3 large eggs
150g/5oz/⅔ cup caster
  (superfine) sugar
150g/5oz/1¼ cups plain
  (all-purpose) flour
5ml/1 tsp vanilla extract
1.5ml/¼ tsp salt
15ml/1 tbsp powdered liquorice

1 Preheat the oven to 180°C/160°C fan/350°F/Gas 4. Grease a 20cm/8in square tin or pan and line with baking parchment.

2 Melt the chocolate and butter in a heatproof bowl set over a pan of simmering (not boiling) water. Set aside to cool slightly.

3 Beat together the eggs and sugar until thick and pale. Stir in the chocolate mixture.

4 Stir in the flour, vanilla and salt until combined, then stir in the powdered liquorice.

5 Pour into the tin and bake for 15–20 minutes until just set but not firm. Cool completely in the tin.

6 Cut into 12–16 pieces when cold. Wrap and store in an airtight container for up to 4 days or freeze (well-wrapped) for up to 4 weeks.

Energy 225kcal/940kJ; Protein 2.9g; Carbohydrate 26.1g, of which sugars 18.8g; Fat 12.8g, of which saturates 7.6g; Cholesterol 57mg; Calcium 33mg; Fibre 0.9g; Sodium 108mg.

Intensely chocolatey, these no-bake crunchy treats make a great gift and are so easy to make. The recipe can be adapted to make different versions: instead of shortbread biscuits you can use amaretti, ginger or digestive biscuits or use dark chocolate to replace the milk chocolate. Don't chop the liquorice too finely – you want to be able to see and taste it.

Liquorice rocky road

MAKES 20–30

300g/11oz plain (semisweet) chocolate, 70% cocoa solids
100g/3½oz milk chocolate, 30% cocoa solids
60ml/4 tbsp golden (light corn) syrup
150g/5oz/⅔ cup unsalted butter
175g/6oz shortbread biscuits or cookies, broken into small pieces
150g/5oz mini marshmallows, pink and white
150g/5oz black liquorice sticks, roughly chopped

1 Line a 23cm/9in square tin or pan with clear film or plastic wrap.

2 Melt the plain and milk chocolate in a pan with the syrup and butter over a low heat, stirring constantly. Remove from the heat and allow to cool slightly.

3 Stir in the shortbread pieces, marshmallows and liquorice then spoon the mixture into the tin. Chill for at least 2 hours until set.

4 Cut into 20–30 small squares. Wrap and store in the refrigerator for up to 1 week.

Energy 170kcal/715kJ; Protein 1.6g; Carbohydrate 20.9g, of which sugars 16g; Fat 9.4g, of which saturates 5.9g; Cholesterol 16mg; Calcium 38mg; Fibre 0.5g; Sodium 36mg.

These striking crisp and dainty macarons are sandwiched together with a creamy white chocolate and liquorice filling. You can make them black if you like – use paste or gel, not liquid food colouring, in the mixture as adding extra liquid will make it too wet. Be careful not to underbake (insides will still be soft) or overbake (they will begin to brown). Delicious served with a cup of tea or coffee.

Liquorice macarons

MAKES 15–20

175g/6oz/1¾ cups icing (confectioners') sugar
125g/4oz/scant 1 cup ground almonds
3 large egg whites
1 pinch salt
75g/3oz/⅓ cup caster (superfine) sugar
black food colouring paste or gel (optional)

FOR THE FILLING
120g/4oz white chocolate, chopped
60ml/2½fl oz/¼ cup double (heavy) cream
50ml/2fl oz/¼ cup sweet liquorice syrup

1 Preheat the oven to 170°C/150°C fan/325°F/Gas 3. Line 2 baking sheets with baking parchment.

2 Blend the icing sugar and ground almonds in a food processor until very fine.

3 Whisk the egg whites with the salt until soft peaks form. Gradually whisk in the caster sugar and colouring, if using, until the mixture is thick. Fold in the almond and icing sugar mixture and mix well.

4 Spoon (or pipe) the mixture into 30–40 small rounds on to the baking sheets. Leave to stand for 20 minutes to form a slight skin.

5 Bake for about 15–18 minutes until firm. Cool on the baking sheets for a few minutes, then place on a wire rack to cool completely.

6 For the filling, put the white chocolate into a heatproof bowl. Bring the double cream and liquorice slowly to the boil in a pan and pour over the chocolate. Stir the mixture until it is smooth and glossy. Leave to cool. Cover and chill for about 2 hours until thick enough to spread.

7 Sandwich the macarons together with the liquorice cream. Store in an airtight container in the refrigerator and eat within 4 days.

Energy 143kcal/601kJ; Protein 2.3g; Carbohydrate 19g, of which sugars 18.2g; Fat 7g, of which saturates 2.4g; Cholesterol 4mg; Calcium 34mg; Fibre 0g; Sodium 19mg.

This delectable cake, flavoured with powdered liquorice, is rich and moist and covered with a lusciously rich chocolate liquorice ganache made with hard black liquorice. It would make a great birthday cake for a liquorice lover. I often make this cake over the Christmas holiday as it makes a pleasant change from the usual rich fruity flavours at this time of year. If you like you can add a teaspoon each of ground cinnamon and ginger for a spicier flavour.

Chocolate liquorice cake

SERVES 6–8

300g/11oz/1⅔ cups dark
  muscovado (molasses) sugar
200ml/7fl oz/scant 1 cup
  boiling water
120g/4oz/½ cup butter
100g/3½oz/scant ½ cup
  caster (superfine) sugar
4 large eggs
240ml/8½fl oz/1 cup sour
  cream
80g/3oz/¾ cup cocoa powder
320g/11½oz/2¾ cups
  self-raising (self-rising) flour
30ml/2 tbsp powdered liquorice
2.5ml/½ tsp bicarbonate of
  soda (baking soda)

FOR THE FILLING AND COATING
1 black liquorice stick, chopped
40ml/2fl oz/¼ cup water
280ml/9½fl oz/generous 1 cup
  double (heavy) cream
15ml/1 tbsp caster (superfine)
  sugar
320g/11½oz plain (semisweet)
  chocolate, 70% cocoa solids
Liquorice allsorts, chopped,
  to decorate

1 Preheat the oven to 180°C/160°C fan/350°F/Gas 4. Grease 2 x 20cm/8in cake tins or pans and line the bases with baking parchment.

2 Mix together the dark muscovado sugar and boiling water until the sugar has dissolved. Set aside.

3 Beat together the butter and caster sugar in a mixing bowl until light and creamy. Add the eggs, sour cream and cocoa powder and beat until smooth.

4 Sift over the flour, liquorice powder and bicarbonate of soda, and fold in gently until smooth and thick. Slowly pour in the muscovado mixture and beat until just incorporated.

5 Divide the mixture evenly between the tins and bake for 25–30 minutes, until a skewer inserted into the centre comes out clean. Cool in the tins for 10 minutes, then place on a wire rack to cool completely.

6 For the filling and coating, heat the liquorice and water in a pan over a medium heat, stirring until the liquorice has almost dissolved. Stir in the cream and heat until very hot, but not boiling. Put the chopped chocolate into a heatproof bowl, pour the hot cream over the chocolate and leave for a few seconds until melted. Beat until smooth and shiny and set aside to cool and thicken until spreadable.

7 Place one cake on to a plate. Spread with a layer of the chocolate cream and place the other cake on top.

8 Spread the remaining chocolate cream over the top and sides of the cake, smoothing with a palette knife. Sprinkle over the chopped liquorice allsorts and leave to set at room temperature. Eat the same day or cover and store in the refrigerator overnight.

Energy 964kcal/4035kJ; Protein 13.2g; Carbohydrate 112.8g, of which sugars 81.6g; Fat 54.4g, of which saturates 32.3g; Cholesterol 216mg; Calcium 268mg; Fibre 4.6g; Sodium 397mg.

This is an interesting departure from traditional fruit cake, with its fabulous combination of tea-soaked dried fruits and treacle. This moist fruit cake is studded with black liquorice, which adds another dimension to the taste. Liquorice tea, made from liquorice root, is widely available and has a sweet, invigorating, aniseed flavour.

Liquorice fruit cake

SERVES 6–8

120ml/4fl oz/½ cup hot
  liquorice tea or black tea
150g/5oz/1 cup mixed raisins
  and currants
150g/5oz/⅔ cup butter
200g/7oz/1 cup light
  muscovado (brown) sugar
300g/11oz/2¾ cups
  self-raising (self-rising) flour
2 eggs, beaten
2.5ml/½ tsp ground cinnamon
15ml/1 tbsp black treacle
  (molasses)
100g/3½oz hard black
  liquorice, roughly chopped
45ml/3 tbsp melted marmalade
Liquorice sweets or candies,
  to decorate

1 Stir together the tea, raisins and currants in a bowl. Cover and leave to soak for at least 20 minutes.

2 Preheat the oven to 170°C/150°C fan/325°F/Gas 3. Grease and line a 20cm/8in round cake tin or pan.

3 Beat the butter and sugar together in a mixing bowl until pale and fluffy. Sift in the flour and add the eggs, mixing until well combined.

4 Pour off half the tea from the dried fruits, then add the remaining tea with the dried fruits to the cake mixture. Stir in the cinnamon, treacle and liquorice.

5 Spoon the mixture into the tin and bake for 25–35 minutes, until a skewer inserted into centre comes out clean. Cool in the tin for 15 minutes then place on a wire rack to cool completely. Brush with melted marmalade and decorate with your choice of liquorice sweets.

6 To store, wrap well and store in an airtight tin for up to 1 month or freeze for up to 3 months.

Energy 490kcal/2064kJ; Protein 6.6g; Carbohydrate 80.9g, of which sugars 50.1g; Fat 17.8g, of which saturates 10.4g; Cholesterol 98mg; Calcium 226mg; Fibre 2.4g; Sodium 313mg.

Rhubarb is an English favourite and this traditional cake with a liquorice twist is a delightful combination of sharp and sweet flavours. It's very versatile – you can eat it cold on its own or spread with butter, or serve it warm as a pudding with liquorice ice cream.

Liquorice & rhubarb loaf

SERVES 6–8

350g/12oz rhubarb, plus ½ stick for topping
200g/7oz/1¾ cups plain (all-purpose) flour
75g/3oz/½ cup wholemeal (whole-wheat) flour
150g/5oz/⅔ cup granulated (white) sugar
2.5ml/½ tsp baking powder
Pinch of salt
15ml/1 tbsp powdered liquorice
75g/3oz/⅓ cup butter
1 egg
200ml/7fl oz/scant 1 cup milk
60g/2½oz/⅓ cup ground almonds

1 Preheat the oven to 180°C/160°C fan/350°F/Gas 4. Remove any fibrous skin from the rhubarb and cut into 2cm/1in lengths. Sprinkle over 30ml/2 tbsp of plain flour and toss to coat the rhubarb.

2 Sift the remaining plain flour into a large mixing bowl, then add the wholemeal flour, sugar, baking powder, salt and powdered liquorice.

3 Melt the butter in a pan, whisk in the egg and milk and stir into the flour mixture. Fold in the ground almonds and rhubarb and pour into a greased 900g/2lb loaf tin or pan. Place the reserved half stick of rhubarb on the top of the mixture.

4 Bake for 60–70 minutes; the cake is cooked when a skewer comes out clean. Leave to rest in the tin for 10 minutes before turning out on to a wire rack to cool.

Energy 330kcal/1388kJ; Protein 7.6g; Carbohydrate 47.2g, of which sugars 22.1g; Fat 13.7g, of which saturates 5.8g; Cholesterol 51mg; Calcium 147mg; Fibre 3g; Sodium 84mg.

This unusual bread can be eaten with savoury or sweet foods. It's particularly nice with cheese. The attractive swirl of dark and light looks good too. It also makes great toast, served with lashings of butter. Use hard black Italian liquorice if you can, for the best flavour.

Liquorice loaf

SERVES 6–8

2 sticks hard black liquorice, chopped
75ml/2½fl oz/⅓ cup water
500g/1¼oz/4½ cups white bread flour
10ml/2 tsp salt
7g/¼oz fast-action yeast
45ml/3 tbsp olive oil
300ml/10fl oz/1¼ cups lukewarm water, more if needed

1 Put the liquorice and water in a heatproof bowl set over a pan of simmering water and leave until melted. Remove from the heat and leave to cool.

2 Put the flour and salt into a large bowl. Stir in the yeast, oil and lukewarm water. Mix until the dough comes together.

3 Turn out on to a lightly floured surface and knead for 10 minutes, until smooth and elastic. Divide the dough in two and mix one half with the liquorice paste.

4 Put the plain and liquorice doughs into lightly oiled bowls and cover with a damp cloth, lightly oiled clear film or plastic wrap. Leave to rise in a warm place for 1–2 hours until doubled in size.

5 Cover a baking sheet with baking parchment.

6 Press the liquorice dough into the white dough to marble. Shape into a loaf and place on the baking sheet. Cover as before and allow to rise in a warm place, until doubled in size.

7 Heat the oven to 200°C/180°C fan/400°F/Gas 6. Bake for 30–40 minutes until risen and cooked through. Cool on a wire rack.

Energy 250kcal/1059kJ; Protein 5.9g; Carbohydrate 48.6g, of which sugars 0.9g; Fat 4.9g, of which saturates 0.7g; Cholesterol 0mg; Calcium 88mg; Fibre 2.6g; Sodium 493mg.

These delicious little cookies have an intriguing flavour and are very easy to make. They keep their shape while cooking and have a lovely texture. You could use different shaped cutters – stars, numbers or people, for a change.

Liquorice cookies

MAKES 20

125g/4oz/½ cup butter
125g/4oz/½ cup caster (superfine) sugar
1 pinch salt
30ml/2 tbsp powdered liquorice
200g/7oz/1¾ cups plain (all-purpose) flour, plus extra for dusting
30–45ml/2–3 tbsp milk
50g/2oz/¾ cup chopped almonds

1 Beat the butter, sugar, salt and liquorice in a mixing bowl until well blended.

2 Add the flour, milk and almonds and mix to a soft dough. Form into a ball, wrap in clear film or plastic wrap and chill for 1 hour.

3 Heat the oven to 180°C/160°C fan/350°F/Gas 4. Line a large baking sheet with baking parchment.

4 Roll out the dough on a lightly floured surface to a thickness of 5mm/¼in.

5 Cut out about 20 rounds with a cookie cutter and place apart on the baking sheet.

6 Bake for 10–15 minutes, until golden brown. Cool on the baking sheet for 5 minutes, then place on a wire rack to cool completely. Store in an airtight container for up to 1 week.

Energy 122kcal/509kJ; Protein 1.7g; Carbohydrate 14.6g, of which sugars 6.9g; Fat 6.7g, of which saturates 3.4g; Cholesterol 13mg; Calcium 34mg; Fibre 0.4g; Sodium 40mg.

Sweets & drinks

Liquorice really comes into its own when making sweets. Home-made sweets taste much better than shop-bought, as they are fresher and made with natural ingredients. And liquorice drinks are wonderfully thirst-quenching, whether hot infusion or cold beverage.

Liquorice adds a new slant to traditional strawberry jam. It's delicious with scones or on toast, or spooned on to a bowl of breakfast porridge or rice pudding. You could also use this jam in a Swiss roll or to sandwich a Victoria sponge cake to add an interesting twist. It should keep in a cool dark place for up to a year.

Strawberry & liquorice jam

MAKES ABOUT 1KG/2¼LB JAM

1kg/2¼lb strawberries
800g/1lb 12oz/1¾ cups jam or
  preserving sugar
60ml/4 tbsp lemon juice
25ml/1½ tbsp powdered
  liquorice

Cook's Tip

Jars must be sterilised and warm before filling them to the brim to allow for shrinkage. Wash the jars in hot soapy water, rinse and put in a low oven to dry and become warm. Stand the jars on folded newspaper to prevent cracking when the hot jam is poured in. Wipe the outside of the filled jars and cover the surface of the jam with waxed paper circles. Seal tightly with lids or transparent covers and elastic bands. This must be done while the jam is hot not warm, to prevent mould forming. Label and store in a cool, dry place.

1 Cut any very large strawberries into smaller pieces to speed up the cooking time. Put the strawberries into a large heavy pan over a low heat and slowly bring to a boil.

2 Reduce the heat and simmer gently for about 10–15 minutes until the fruit has softened.

3 Add the sugar, lemon juice and liquorice and stir over a low heat until the sugar has dissolved completely.

4 Bring to the boil and boil rapidly for about 15–20 minutes until setting point is reached, 105°C/220°F on a sugar thermometer. To tell when setting point has been reached, remove the pan from the heat and put a little of the boiling mixture on a chilled saucer. As it cools, the jam will begin to set and will wrinkle when pushed gently with your finger and will remain in two separate parts when you draw your finger through it. It is a good idea to have ready 3 or 4 saucers in the freezer or refrigerator for testing the jam.

5 Skim off any foam and allow the jam to cool for 15 minutes, to ensure the strawberries are distributed evenly.

6 Pour into warm sterilised jars, cover, seal and label.

Energy 3422kcal/14570kJ; Protein 9.6g; Carbohydrate 900g, of which sugars 900g; Fat 1.4g, of which saturates 0g; Cholesterol 0mg; Calcium 385mg; Fibre 14.7g; Sodium 100mg.

These meltingly rich truffles are very moreish and easy to make. Rolling them in liquorice powder adds even more liquorice flavour. You could press a small liquorice sweet on top of the truffles before chilling, for extra decoration. Serve them with coffee as an after-dinner treat – or just enjoy them on their own!

Chocolate liquorice truffles

MAKES ABOUT 30

225g/8oz plain (semisweet)
   chocolate, 70% cocoa solids
45ml/3 tbsp unsalted butter
150ml/5fl oz/⅔ cup double
   (heavy) cream
15ml/1 tbsp powdered liquorice

TO FINISH
55–65g/2–3oz/½–¾ cup
   cocoa powder or powdered
   liquorice

1 Put the chocolate, butter and cream in a heatproof bowl set over a pan of simmering (not boiling) water until the chocolate has melted. Stir until smooth.

2 Stir in the liquorice and leave to cool, then cover and chill in the refrigerator for 2–3 hours until firm.

3 Roll small pieces of the mixture into about 30 x 2.5cm/1in balls. If the mixture becomes too soft to roll, return to the refrigerator to firm up.

4 Roll the truffles in the cocoa or liquorice powder and chill until firm. Store in an airtight container in the refrigerator for up to 1 week.

Energy 80kcal/331kJ; Protein 0.8g; Carbohydrate 5.1g, of which sugars 4.8g; Fat 6.4g, of which saturates 3.9g; Cholesterol 11mg; Calcium 10mg; Fibre 0.5g; Sodium 19mg.

My own particular favourite – gorgeous chewy toffee complemented by the bittersweet tang of liquorice. This takes me back to my childhood on Bonfire Night when we children enjoyed tucking into a bag of mysteriously dark liquorice toffee. If you want a stronger flavour, replace half the golden syrup with black treacle.

Liquorice toffee

MAKES ABOUT 64 PIECES

125g/4oz/½ cup unsalted
   butter
225g/8oz/1 cup granulated
   (white) sugar
200g/7oz/scant 1 cup
   sweetened condensed milk
175ml/6fl oz/¾ cup golden
   (light corn) syrup
Pinch of salt
10ml/2 tsp powdered liquorice
1.5ml/¼ tsp black food
   colouring paste or gel

1 Grease a 20cm/8in square baking tin or pan, then line with baking parchment and grease again.

2 Place the butter, sugar, condensed milk and golden syrup in a deep, heavy pan over a very low heat, stirring constantly until the sugar has dissolved completely.

3 Increase the heat slightly and bring to the boil. Cook, stirring constantly to 118°C/245°F on a sugar thermometer.

4 Remove from the heat and stir in the salt, liquorice and food colouring. Beat the mixture well until the black paste colours it evenly.

5 Pour into the tin and leave to cool for 1 hour, then chill overnight until set.

6 Cut into small pieces and wrap in cellophane or baking parchment. Store in an airtight container for up to 2 weeks.

Energy 46kcal/196kJ; Protein 0.3g; Carbohydrate 7.6g, of which sugars 7.6g; Fat 1.9g, of which saturates 1.2g; Cholesterol 5mg; Calcium 11mg; Fibre 0g; Sodium 12mg.

You can't beat homemade fudge with its melt-in-the-mouth creamy, crumbly-yet-soft texture that makes it very moreish. It makes a brilliant gift, packed into attractive boxes or bags. Liquorice adds its unique, distinctive flavour to this delicious fudge. Different brands of liquorice essence vary in strength so do start by adding the smaller amount.

Liquorice fudge

Store in an airtight container for up to 2 weeks.

MAKES 20–30 PIECES

110g/4oz/½ cup butter, plus extra for greasing
800g/1¾lb/4 cups soft light brown sugar
300ml/11fl oz/1⅓ cups milk
5–10ml/1–2 tsp natural liquorice essence
Few drops black food colouring, optional

1 Butter a 20–23cm/8–9in square tin or pan.

2 Put the butter, sugar and milk into a heavy pan and heat gently, stirring constantly until the sugar has dissolved completely.

3 Increase the heat and slowly bring to the boil. Boil steadily for 20–25 minutes, until a little of the mixture can be rolled into a soft ball between your finger and thumb when dropped into cold water (115°C/238°F on a sugar thermometer).

4 Remove from the heat and stir in the liquorice essence and colouring, if using. Allow to stand for 5 minutes, then beat well until the mixture grains and becomes thick and creamy. Pour into the tin and cut into squares when set.

Energy 137kcal/580kJ; Protein 0.4g; Carbohydrate 28.5g, of which sugars 28.5g; Fat 3.2g, of which saturates 2g; Cholesterol 9mg; Calcium 14mg; Fibre 0g; Sodium 29mg.

An old Scottish recipe from the countryside, this delicious treat bears a slightly strange name, but the flavour and texture are delightful. In the old sweetshops of Scotland, the 'sweetie wives', as the shopkeepers were called, would have made these with ground ginger. If you can obtain whole liquorice root and a spice grinder for this recipe, the resulting taste is wonderful.

Mealie candy

MAKES ABOUT 750G/1LB 11OZ

Butter, for greasing
75g/3oz oatmeal or jumbo oats, ground in a food processor
400g/14oz/2 cups caster (superfine) sugar
200ml/7fl oz/scant 1 cup water
100g/3¾oz black treacle (molasses)
2.5ml/½ tsp powdered liquorice

Cook's Tip

The combination of nutritious oatmeal, iron-rich black treacle and a hint of liquorice, means this confection actually has some health benefits.

1 Preheat the oven to 180°C/160°C fan/350°C/Gas 4. Line a baking sheet with baking parchment and grease with a little butter. Set aside.

2 Spread the oatmeal out on another baking sheet and toast for 10 minutes, until it is golden. Keep a close eye on it.

3 Put the sugar, water and treacle in a heavy pan, heat gently until the sugar dissolves, then boil for 10 minutes. Gently stir in the toasted oatmeal and liquorice.

4 Pour the mixture into the prepared baking sheet. Leave to cool completely.

5 Turn out on to a board and cut into circles or squares.

6 Serve immediately, or wrap the sweets individually in baking parchment and store in an airtight container at room temperature for up to 3 weeks.

Energy 2134kcal/9094kJ; Protein 12.7g; Carbohydrate 539.8g, of which sugars 484.8g; Fat 6.6g, of which saturates 0g; Cholesterol 0mg; Calcium 722mg; Fibre 6.8g; Sodium 225mg.

This is a hard version of liquorice, to suck on rather than chew. The bicarbonate of soda lightens the texture a little, so the shards are slightly brittle.

Liquorice shards

MAKES ABOUT 550G/1LB 4OZ

Butter, for greasing
200g/7oz/1 cup caster (superfine) sugar
100g/3¾oz golden (light corn) syrup
100g/3¾oz black treacle (molasses)
100ml/3½fl oz/scant ½ cup water
2.5ml/½ tsp cream of tartar
1 liquorice root, pounded
5ml/1 tsp powdered liquorice or 2.5–5ml/½–1 tsp essence
65g/2½oz liquid fruit pectin or 12g/¼oz powdered fruit pectin
2.5ml/½ tsp bicarbonate of soda (baking soda)
2.5ml/½ tsp salt
5ml/1 tsp anise extract

1 Grease a 23cm/9in square cake tin or pan and line with clear film or plastic wrap as smoothly as possible.

2 Combine the sugar, golden syrup, black treacle, water and cream of tartar in a heavy pan. Stir over a low heat until the sugar has dissolved. Add the liquorice root and liquorice powder or essence, and boil, without stirring, until it reaches 120°C/248°F.

3 In a separate bowl, combine the pectin (add 60ml/4 tbsp water if using powdered pectin), bicarbonate of soda and salt.

4 Pour the pectin mixture into the syrup and stir to combine. Boil again until the syrup reaches 103°C/217°F, then stir in the anise extract.

5 Pour the syrup into the prepared tin, discarding the liquorice root, and leave to set for about 4 hours. Turn out on to a chopping board and break into shapes. Serve immediately, or store in an airtight container for up to 3 weeks.

Energy 1343kcal/5727kJ; Protein 8.8g; Carbohydrate 355.2g, of which sugars 354.8g; Fat 1.7g, of which saturates 0g; Cholesterol 0mg; Calcium 1204mg; Fibre 0g; Sodium 1442mg.

A favourite with children and adults alike all over the world, liquorice sticks are delectable eaten on their own, or you could dip them in sherbet. You can make these the traditional way with anise oil and some black food colouring, or you can make red liquorice sticks and omit the liquorice anise. You can wrap the sticks individually in waxed paper or line a pretty box with paper and place them inside.

Liquorice sticks

MAKES ABOUT 20

125g/4¼oz/generous ½ cup butter, plus extra for greasing
400g/14oz/2 cups caster (superfine) sugar
400g/14oz sweetened condensed milk
250ml/8fl oz/1 cup golden (light corn) syrup
0.75ml/⅛ tsp salt
5ml/1 tsp powdered liquorice or 2.5–5ml/½–1 tsp essence
5ml/1 tsp anise extract (omit this for red liquorice sticks)
2.5ml/½ tsp black food colouring paste (or red for red liquorice sticks)

1 Line a 23cm/9in square baking tin or pan with foil. Extend the foil over the edges of the tin. Grease the foil.

2 Melt the butter in a large, heavy pan. Add the caster sugar, sweetened condensed milk, golden syrup and salt. Stir well until the sugar dissolves.

3 Boil the mixture at a steady, moderate rate over a medium heat, stirring frequently, until it reaches the firm-ball stage (120°C/248°F). This should take 15–20 minutes. The mixture scorches easily so scrape the bottom of the pan well when you stir it to prevent the mixture from sticking.

4 Remove from the heat. Add the liquorice powder or essence, anise extract (if using) and the food colouring to the pan.

5 Quickly pour the mixture, without scraping, into the prepared tin. Cool for several hours or until firm. Use the foil to lift the liquorice out of the tin and on to a chopping board. Peel away and discard the foil.

6 Using a buttered sharp knife, cut the mixture into 1cm/½in wide strips. Store for up to 1 month.

Energy 229kcal/967kJ; Protein 1.9g; Carbohydrate 41.9g, of which sugars 41.9g; Fat 7.2g, of which saturates 4.5g; Cholesterol 21mg; Calcium 68mg; Fibre 0g; Sodium 101mg.

These little liquorice drops are intensified by the addition of two types of anise: the oil from the anise seed, and the seeds and seed-pod of the star anise. The combination creates a punchy old-fashioned black liquorice flavour. The salt is inspired by Danish salt liquorice, though this version contains less salt as it can be rather overpowering.

Liquorice star anise drops

MAKES ABOUT 24

Butter, for greasing
200g/7oz/1 cup caster (superfine) sugar
100g/3¾oz golden (light corn) syrup
100g/3¾oz black treacle (molasses)
100ml/3½fl oz/scant ½ cup water
2.5ml/½ tsp cream of tartar
5ml/1 tsp powdered liquorice or 2.5–5ml/½–1 tsp essence
3 star anise
65g/2½oz liquid fruit pectin or 15g/½oz powdered fruit pectin
2.5ml/½ tsp salt
5ml/1 tsp anise extract
Sea salt, to sprinkle on top

1 Grease a baking sheet and line with baking parchment or clear film or plastic wrap, ensuring it is as smooth as possible.

2 Combine the sugar, golden syrup, black treacle, water and cream of tartar in a heavy pan. Stir over low heat to dissolve the sugar, then add the liquorice powder or essence and star anise and bring to the boil. Boil until it reaches hard-ball stage (130°C/266°F).

3 In a separate bowl, combine the pectin (add 60ml/4 tbsp water if using powdered pectin) and salt.

4 Pour the pectin into the syrup and stir to combine. Continue to stir to avoid the possibility of the syrup boiling over.

5 Bring to the boil again until the syrup reaches the firm-ball stage (120°C/248°F). Immediately remove from the heat. Stir in the anise extract. Remove and discard the star anise.

6 Pour the syrup on to the prepared sheet in drops. Sprinkle with sea salt. Leave them to set for 4 hours. Serve immediately or store in an airtight container for up to 3 weeks.

Energy 66kcal/283kJ; Protein 0.1g; Carbohydrate 17.6g, of which sugars 16.4g; Fat 0g, of which saturates 0g; Cholesterol 0mg; Calcium 5mg; Fibre 0g; Sodium 27mg.

These soft and intense liquorice cakes are based on the originals from Pontefract, England, which date back to the 17th century. Originally, a seal with a depiction of Pontefract Castle was applied to the top of each cake. If you have some little madeleine, tartlet or jelly moulds, try using the bottom of those. Or, if you have a wax seal stamp, that would look appealing.

Pontefract-style cakes

MAKES ABOUT 550G/1LB 4OZ

100g/3¾oz butter, plus extra
  for greasing
200g/7oz/1 cup caster
  (superfine) sugar
75ml/5 tbsp golden (light corn)
  syrup
45ml/3 tbsp black treacle
  (molasses)
120ml/8 tbsp sweetened
  condensed milk
2.5ml/½ tsp salt
5ml/1 tsp powdered liquorice or
  2.5–5ml/½–1 tsp essence
7.5ml/1½ tsp anise extract
A few drops of black food
  colouring
5ml/1 tsp bicarbonate of soda
  (baking soda)

1 Grease a 23 x 33cm/9 x 13in baking sheet and line with baking parchment.

2 Place all of the ingredients in a heavy pan. Heat gently, stirring, until dissolved.

3 Turn up the heat and bring the syrup up to 112°C/233°F, stirring constantly, without scraping down the sides of pan.

4 Pour the mixture into the prepared sheet. Leave to cool, then chill for 10 minutes.

5 Remove from the refrigerator and stamp out small rounds with a small plain pastry or cookie cutter. Transfer the rounds to a sheet of baking parchment.

6 Press the tops of the cakes with a stamp or mould. Serve immediately, or wrap in waxed paper and store in an airtight container for 1 month.

Energy 2271kcal/9553kJ; Protein 12.9g; Carbohydrate 365.7g, of which sugars 365.5g; Fat 94.4g, of which saturates 59.7g; Cholesterol 256mg; Calcium 713mg; Fibre 0g; Sodium 3145mg.

This delicious easy-to-make smoothie is bursting with fruit and is healthy, nutritious and refreshing. Ring the changes by substituting the same weight of different berries such as blueberries, blackberries, redcurrants, etc. Instead of plain yogurt you could use flavoured.

Liquorice berry smoothie

SERVES 4

150ml/5fl oz/⅔ cup plain or natural yogurt
2 very ripe bananas
300g/11oz strawberries and raspberries, mixed
300ml/11fl oz/1⅓ cups milk
10–15ml/2–3 tsp sweet liquorice syrup

1 Put all the ingredients in a food processor or blender and blend until smooth.

2 Pour into chilled glasses and serve immediately.

Energy 126kcal/533kJ; Protein 5.5g; Carbohydrate 23.4g, of which sugars 21.8g; Fat 1.8g, of which saturates 1.1g; Cholesterol 6mg; Calcium 158mg; Fibre 1.8g; Sodium 66mg.

This refreshing ancient beverage is an infusion of erk sous (liquorice root) in water; the mixture is then strained and chilled before serving. No sugar is added, as liquorice is naturally sweet. It's been a favourite drink in Egypt, Syria and Morocco for centuries. In the street markets, sellers in traditional outfits, clanking cymbals, carry the drink in metal containers on their backs and serve it in small cups. The drink's original colour is light brown but turns dark as it ferments, due to a chemical reaction of the bicarbonate of soda and water.

Sharab al-eriq sous

SERVES 6–8

50g/2oz liquorice roots, crushed
2 pinches bicarbonate of soda
   (baking soda)
1.2 litres/2 pints/5 cups water
5–10ml/1–2 tsp orange flower
   water, optional

1 Put the liquorice roots in a bowl and sprinkle with bicarbonate of soda. Add 50ml/2fl oz/¼ cup of water and mix with your hand until the liquorice roots are moistened. Cover and set aside overnight in a warm place.

2 Spread the moistened liquorice roots on a large piece of muslin or cheesecloth. Wrap the cloth to enclose the roots and put the cloth in a jug or pitcher. Add 500ml/18fl oz/generous 2 cups water to the jug. Cover and chill in the refrigerator for 24 hours.

3 Remove the cloth from the jug and discard the roots. Add the remaining water to the jug and orange flower water to taste, if using.

4 Pour the drink from a height into another jug. This will produce the characteristic foam.

5 Repeat the pouring several times, then pour from a height into chilled glasses and serve immediately.

Energy 6kcal/negkJ; Protein 3.1g; Carbohydrate 0g, of which sugars 0g; Fat 0.8g, of which saturates 0g; Cholesterol 0mg; Calcium 90mg; Fibre 0g; Sodium 821mg.

Index